Real Ghost Stories Haunted UK - True Ghost and Paranormal Stories

Carole Somerville

Copyright © by Carole Somerville, 2017

This book should not be sold, reproduced, copied, loaned or hired out, or otherwise circulated without the writer's prior consent in any form of binding or cover other than that in which it is published.

Photographs: C Somerville, H Somerville, C West and L Webb

ISBN-13:
978-1539064145
ISBN-10:
153906414X

Contents

Introduction
Part (i)
Haunted Castles in the UK ... page 8
Chillingham Castle: Most Haunted Place on Earth
... page 9
Ghosts and Vampire of Alnwick Castle, Northumberland
... page 13
The Pink Lady of Bamburgh Castle
... page 15
Ghostly Monk of Lindisfarne Castle
... page 17
The Grey Lady of Warkworth Castle
... page 19
The Viking Ghost of Tynemouth Castle
... page 21
The Green Lady of Comlongon Castle, Dumfries, Scotland
... page 22
Haunted Castles in the UK
... page 26
Part (ii)
Hauntings, Poltergeists and Supernatural Beings
... page 59
Poltergeists and Ghosts
... page 63
The Epworth Rectory Poltergeist
... page 63
Anonymous Ghosts
... page 67
Ghostly Presences
... page 68

Familial and Famous Ghosts
… page 69

Famous Ghosts: Mary Queen of Scots
… page 70
Famous Ghosts: Dick Turpin
… page 72
Animal Hauntings
The Demon Cat of Killakee
… page 76
Phantom Dog of Dublin
… page 79
Dublin's Dolocher
… page 80
Greyfriars Bobby
… page 82
Real Ghost Stories of Ghostly Sightings
Ghosts of Northumbria – Who is Silky?
… page 86
Haunted Places and Haunted Vessels
… page 88
Haunted Ships on the Solway
… page 91
Haunted Places – Ghosts of Huntington Castle
… page 93
Ghostly spirits of Skryne Castle
… page 95
Wicked Jimmy: the Ghost of Lowther Castle
… page 97
Haunted Edinburgh
… page 99
The Ghostly Mary King's Close
… page 100
The Ghost of Cartmel Fell, Cumbria
… page 101

Phantom Islands
... page 103
Orbs, Spears and Globes of Light on Videos and
Photographs
... page 108
Angels, Fairies and Supernatural Beings
... page 112
Dobbies (elves) of Cumbria
... page 114
Ghostly Giants
... page 115
Ghosts of St Michael's Mount, Cornwall
... page 117
Ghostly Angels
... page 119

Part (iii)
Amazing Paranormal Stories and Investigations
... page 121
Taking Part in Ghost Hunts
... page 121
How is Paranormal Activity Investigated?
... page 123
Amazing Paranormal Stories and Investigations:
Haunted Cinemas and Theatres in the UK
... page 127
Paranormal Investigations at Mary King's Close,
Edinburgh
... page 133
Paranormal Investigations: The Schooner Hotel,
Alnmouth, Northumberland
... page 142
Supernatural Activity at Jedburgh Castle Jail
... page 146

Paranormal Investigations: Edlingham Castle,
Northumberland
... page 149
Haunted Muncaster Castle
... page 152
Haunted Kielder Castle, Northumberland
... page 155
Chillingham Castle the Most Haunted Location in England
... page 158
Culzean Castle Ghosts
... page 160
How to tell if your house is haunted
... page 162

Part (iv)
True Ghost and Paranormal Stories
Ghost in a Cake Shop
... page 168
Haunted Roads in the UK
... page 184
Haunted Trains and Railway Stations
... page 193
Haunted Carlisle
... page 196
The Cursing Stone – Can a Whole City be Cursed?
... page 199
The Ghost of Talkin Tarn
... page 206
The Brampton Witch
... page 209
The Croglin Vampire
... page 212
Haunted Hospitals and Care homes
... page 214

Angelic Paranormal Activity
... page 220
Granddad is Never Far Away
... page 226
The Ghost Village of Imber
... page 229
Haunted Chagford
... page 232
Radiant Boys
... page 235
Angel Encounter
... page 237
Hotel Hauntings
... page 239
Haunted Boscastle Hotel
... page 244
Not all Ghosts are Evil
... page 248

Introduction

Whether or not you believe in ghosts, you've likely shown interest at some time in your life in a ghostly tale or two. Or you may have found yourself looking twice at a photograph where a ghostly figure cannot be explained. Some buildings and places seem to attract ghostly presences which have explanations. Other hauntings are mysterious and cannot be explained. This book is an amalgamation of my "Haunted" series. Part 1 will take you on a tour of some of the most haunted castles, inns and mansions in the UK. Part 2 looks at the different types of ghosts and hauntings with more true ghost story examples. Read about haunted theatres, castles, underground bunkers and buried streets in Part 3 and more spooky tales are included in Part 4.

Drawn from literary and internet sources, local records and folk legends as well as personal visits and interviews, this is a chilly collection of some hauntingly romantic, some gruesome and other eerie tales of ghosts, ghouls and animal spirits that walk the Earth

So, turn out the light, snuggle up by the fire and get ready to read some spine-chilling ghostly tales of the unexpected.

Part (i)
Haunted Castles in the UK

North, south, east or west, almost every corner of the UK can boast of having its haunted castle. Many of these ancient buildings have a sinister and gruesome past and most have built up a reputation of being haunted.

Some offer tours through their dark rooms and shadowy, narrow stone passageways where paranormal activity has been experienced, eerie presences felt or ghostly figures seen.

As well as ghost tours, for those who are very brave, some castles such as Chillingham Castle in Northumberland offer the chance of joining in all-night ghostly vigils.

Chillingham Castle: Is this the most haunted place on Earth?

Chillingham, with its ghostly rooms and dark dungeon is said, by some, to be the most haunted place on earth. Here, in its torture chamber, many thousands of Scots were tortured to death.

Entry to the castle grounds is through a heavy set of gates, designed to deter trespassers when closed and when opened invites brave visitors to enter onto the road that leads to the castle. Part of this path is known as the Devil's Walk and this is where a group of Scots were attacked and killed. Apparently their bodies were left along the path, scattered and decaying, as a warning to anyone who might be thinking about trying to enter or take over Chillingham Castle. As well as the ghosts of the Scots, another ghost that haunts the Devil's Walk and the castle is that of John Sage whose nickname was 'Dragfoot' due to a spear injury that had torn a ligament in one of his feet during a battle with the Scottish. The injury left his foot useless and his military career over.

Now very few men would take on the next job he was offered but John Sage being the hideous person that he was jumped at the chance of a position of Chillingham Castle torturer. Such a gruesome job appealed to this vile man's macabre nature and it is said that over a period of three years he tortured at least fifty Scots a week. Of all the people visiting Chillingham in medieval times, it has been estimated that only three per-cent came out alive. John Sage carried out some of the most hideous tortures in history using a number of horrific devises including branding irons, a rack, leg irons, a bed of nails and a boiling pot.

With no windows for air and with 50 Scots being tortured to death every week, imagine the rotten smell of decaying bodies that must have filled the air!

Talk about reaping what you sow and Sage himself met as gruesome an end as the Scots he had got so much pleasure out of torturing. He is said to have accidentally strangled his lover Elizabeth Charlton, while they were making love on the rack. Elizabeth's father, a clan leader, demanded that the castle owner have Sage killed or he would join with the Scots in an attack against the Castle. Chillingham Castle's owner, Edward Longshank ordered that Sage be hanged in the castle grounds on the Devil's Mile. A crowd of jeering onlookers watched the hanging and apparently while he was still alive, set to slicing his body to pieces. According to some tales they took parts of his body: toes, fingers, ears and even his testicles as souvenirs.

The ghost of this evil man still haunts the Devil's Walk and Sage has also been heard and sensed within the castle.

Those who have witnessed his ghost reported hearing the sound of dragging footsteps due to his mutilated leg. His ghost is also linked with a dirty putrid stench and a feeling of being watched or being pushed.

Also within the castle grounds, several ghostly sightings have been witnessed in the garden area and courtyard whilst perhaps one of the most chilling visions reported is that of a phantom funeral procession.

Eerie moans and whimpering have been heard by visitors to the castle. These, it is said, are the cries of the Blue Boy whose bones along with blue scraps of clothing were discovered behind a wall.

According to some tales, it is when midnight strikes that visitors are most likely to hear the Blue Boy's disturbing wails coming from an area that was once a part of the ten-foot thick wall in the pink bedroom. This section of the wall was cut through to make a passage. In the early 1900s, visitors spending the night in this bedroom reported firstly hearing a young child's eerie cries which would suddenly stop. Then in the silence, they saw a thin young boy, dressed in blue and surrounded by a bright halo of light, approach the old four-poster bed.

It was while some building work was being carried out in the 1920s that the bones of a child along with the remaining scraps of a blue garment were discovered within the wall. The skeleton was interred in the local graveyard and although the boy himself has ceased to make an appearance, those who are brave enough to sleep in the Pink Bedroom have reported seeing flashes of blue light centred on one particular wall, after midnight.

As well as the chilling moans of this tortured child, other ghosts that haunt Chillingham castle include a wandering lady in white, voices in the chapel and the spirit of Lady Mary

Berkeley whose steps and the rustle of her dress can be heard on the turret stairs.

This ghostly Lady's husband, Lord Grey of Wark and Chillingham, apparently caused some scandal in the area during the early 1600s by running off with her sister, Henrietta. They left the distraught Lady Mary abandoned at the castle with her baby. She fell into a deep depression and now her spirit wanders the corridors of Chillingham in search of her cheating husband. Some say she steps out of her portrait to wander the castle late at night.

A frail ghostly woman dressed in white has been seen in the inner-pantry of the castle. This ghost not only haunts Chillingham with her eerie appearance but she speaks to people, too. A watchman was sleeping in the room one night, guarding the silver that was once stored there. He noticed a woman had approached him and naturally thought she was a guest at the castle. When she asked him for some water, he turned to get her some and then suddenly remembered that the door was locked and no-one could have therefore entered. As he turned, he discovered she had vanished.

A psychic who once visited the castle who claimed to have had no prior knowledge of its history, sensed a woman in the pantry who was thirsty and felt the woman may have been poisoned.

Many people have heard two men, apparently deep in conversation, in the library underneath the upper chamber and yet no-one has been able to distinguish what was being said. This is because the moment anyone consciously stops reading or writing to try to listen to them, they stop talking!

Chillingham Castle offers regular ghost tours of the castle and the grounds all year round by arrangement but this not the only haunted castle in Northumberland. In fact for anyone planning a ghost-hunting holiday in the UK, Northumberland could well be the place for you. Situated on the border of England and Scotland, Northumberland is the scene of some of the most violent and dramatic events in UK history. This county has witnessed many blood-thirsty battles, it has more castles than any other in England and most are said to be haunted.

Ghosts and Vampire of Alnwick Castle, Northumberland

Alnwick Castle is likely to be the one most people are familiar with. This magnificent castle which dominates the surrounding countryside has been used as a film location for *Harry Potter*, *Blackadder*, *Elizabeth* and *Robin Hood Prince of*

Thieves. Also known as the "Windsor of the North", this ancient castle has been perched on the English/Scottish Border for more than one thousand years.

One of the castle's servants is said to have once haunted Alnwick and he wasn't a pleasant fellow. He did not treat his wife well so it wouldn't be surprising if rumours spread around the castle about her being unfaithful were true. Inevitably, the tales got back to the husband and when he heard his wife was having an affair, he decided to hide above the bed to catch her in the act. Whether or not his suspicions were proven correct wouldn't have mattered to him for much longer, as apparently he fell and he must have injured himself very badly because the next day, he died! After his burial his ghost was seen wandering aimlessly around the streets of Alnwick.

Coincidence perhaps, but at the time his ghost was seen, a sickness came over the community. Many people died. Concerned about the link between the ghostly sightings and this dreadful illness that had struck so many, a meeting of town leaders was called. It was agreed that the local Priest lead the group to the cemetery to dig up this fellow's grave. When the casket was opened, according to legend, blood began to ooze from the body. The group instantly ordered that it be burned. The sickness that had spread so quickly through the market town of Alnwick vanished soon after this and seemingly the ghost was never seen again. So maybe the ghost sighting and the sickness had been linked!

Rumour also tells of a vampire that once lived at Alnwick castle. He dwelled underneath this magnificent building. Sunlight, it is said, kills vampires and this particular vampire – who is reputed to have once been a Lord of the Estate – would come out at night to roam the castle grounds and nearby town of Alnwick, attacking unsuspecting locals. Coincidentally, an outbreak of the plague was also attributed to this vampire and the consequence? – A group of townspeople dug up the vampire, removed him from his shallow grave and burned the unholy creature.

Could it be therefore that the supernatural creatures in both these legends relate to one and the same being?

Just thirty minutes' drive from Alnwick will take you to Bamburgh Castle on the coast. This formidable castle with magnificent coastal views stands majestically on a rocky outcrop above the village below. It has a rugged history of bloody battles, royal rebellion and resident ghosts and has been used in its time as a girls' school, a granary and as a home for shipwrecked sailors. The Armstrong family live in this castle along with its resident ghosts, the Pink Lady, the Green Lady and a Knight. It is open to the public.

The Pink Lady of Bamburgh Castle

The Pink Lady is believed to have been a Princess who fell in love with a man her father disapproved of. The King agreed to the marriage but there was a condition: he ordered that the young man be sent away for seven years. If they were still in love and wanted to be together on his return, the couple could marry. The King forbade the young lovers to exchange communications during that time in the hope that their passion would cool.

But much to the King's disappointment, the princess patiently waited at Bamburgh all those long years. And although he could see she was not happy and longed for the youth's return, her father was determined to get her to give up hope of seeing him again. So just before the seven years was up, he told her that his spies had informed him the sweetheart she was pining for had married someone else, overseas.

The princess was distraught and to try to cheer her up, the King ordered a seamstress to make a gown for the princess in her favourite shade of pink. When it arrived, the princess had her maids help her dress in the lovely pink gown before she made her way up the stairway to the highest battlements and threw herself to her doom.

The King of course had lied to her and the lover returned a single man not long afterwards. Every seven years since the day of her death, the pink ghost is said to visit Bamburgh Castle, gliding through the corridors and visiting the battlements to stare out towards the sea watching and waiting for her lover's return.

She has also been seen on the rocky path leading to the shore and standing on the beach gazing out to sea, hoping to catch a glimpse of her lost love.

Anyone who hears clanking or the occasional rattle of chains in the corridors of Bamburgh might also see the Old Knight in armour who regularly visits the castle. Whilst the spiral staircase is known to be haunted by the Green Lady. She has been seen carrying a bundle of rags which are believed to be her baby. Some say the young woman in green was a starving pauper who once visited the castle begging for bread from the guards. Instead of taking pity on her plight, they took advantage of her, and so the story goes, in her weakened state, she stumbled and fell down the staircase to her death.

Ghostly Monk of Lindisfarne Castle

Not far from Bamburgh is the picturesque Holy Island which can only be accessed from the mainland by car along the causeway when the tide is out. Majestically perched on the volcanic mound known as Beblowe Craig, Lindisfarne Castle commands the view from miles around.

St Cuthbert, born in Northumbria around AD 635 lived at Holy Island (or Lindisfarne as it was then called) during his thirties. Here he ran a monastery and was an active missionary with the power of spiritual healing and ability, so it is said, to work miracles. At the age of forty he lived as a hermit on a more remote island called the Inner Farne although he was visited regularly by those who sought spiritual guidance.

At the age of fifty the King and the church requested that he come out of retirement to become bishop of Hexham to which he reluctantly agreed. St Cuthbert journeyed throughout the land in this role but returned to the Hermitage on Farne Island just before his death where in the company of the Lindisfarne Monks, he died in 687 AD. His body was buried in his monastery at Lindisfarne and he was celebrated for his remarkable miracles.

Eleven years after his death, during a transfer of relics, astonished Monks of the island found his body was still in a fresh and incorrupt state, a certain sign that he was a saint. Pilgrims still flock to Lindisfarne in huge numbers as they did in Cuthbert's lifetime. This beautiful island has the most peaceful and serene atmosphere. There are many churches dedicated to St Cuthbert in England and Scotland. His body has been in Durham since 995.

St Cuthbert's ghost, dressed in a simple brown robe, is said to wander through the ancient ruins of Lindisfarne Priory. His ghostly spirit is more likely to be seen on the night of a Full Moon when the causeway is cut off from the mainland by the tide. Rumours also speak of St Cuthbert's ghost being heard working a hammer to make holes in stones called Cuthbert's Beads which are found locally and used for rosaries to bring luck for those who carry them.

Henry VIII built Lindisfarne Castle (now in the care of the National Trust) in the 1550s using stones from the demolished Priory. St Cuthbert's ghost is also known to haunt the area around the castle. These rocks are also haunted by a soldier who is believed to have resided there during the English Civil War when there was an attack on the castle.

There are other phantom Monks said to haunt the island. Some have been seen walking across the causeway. One ghostly Monk was seen within the castle itself before disappearing through a wall while a soldier from Cromwell's time has also been witnessed within Lindisfarne Castle.

Of St Cuthbert's Ghost, it is said that he once visited Alfred the Great while he was a fugitive at the castle. According to this story the ghostly Monk appeared before Alfred and told him that all would be well and Alfred would one day sit on the throne of England. – The ghost's prediction eventually did come true.

The Grey Lady of Warkworth Castle

Standing on the English/Scotland border is Warkworth Castle now an impressive ancient ruin. This area was the scene of many a raging conflict as it switched ownership between the English and the Scots many times throughout its history.

Warkworth Castle's resident ghost which has been seen wandering around its towers is known as the Grey Lady. She is believed, by some, to be Margaret Neville, wife of Henry Percy the first Earl of Northumberland. Others say the ghost is Isabel Widdrington whose father was the Lord of Widdrington Castle, situated close to Warkworth.

According to legend, Sir Bertram of Bothal Castle had fallen in love with the beautiful Isabel. During a feast at Alnwick Castle Sir Bertram was presented with an engraved helmet and was told that to win her hand in marriage he had to wear the helmet "bravely in battle." Soon afterwards, Sir Bertram was given the chance to test the helmet in battle in a bloody conflict against the Scots.

He was seriously wounded and taken back to the castle at Wark to recuperate. Isabel was horrified when she heard that he had been injured and felt guilty about the part she had played in his injury. Immediately on hearing the news she set out on horseback to nurse him. But on the journey she had an unfortunate encounter and was carried off by a Scottish Chief.

When Isabel did not show up at Wark, the worried Sir Bertram left his bed to journey the Borderlands in search of his lost love. He discovered she was being held prisoner in the castle of a notorious Border Raider and made his way there to rescue her.

Arriving in the dead of night, Sir Bertram just happened to witness his Lady Love fleeing the castle with a man dressed in tartan. He followed them and demanded that the Scotsman should release Isabel. Angry and mad with anxiety to rescue his love, Sir Bertram attacked the man with his sword. As he fell to the ground and Sir Bertram raised his sword to strike again, Isabel threw herself between them to receive the full force of the sword.

She fell to the ground and used her dying words to explain how Sir Bertram's brother, disguised as a Scot, had arranged to help her escape the castle. Sir Bertram was distraught with grief. In a panic-stricken moment he had killed his own brother and the woman he had hoped to marry.

In grief and remorse, Bertram returned to Northumberland where he found sanctuary at Warkworth Castle. He gave away all his wealth for the building of churches and hospitals and carved out the cave now known as the Hermitage at Warkworth.

Within this cave that is situated on the banks of the river not far from Warkworth, is a small chapel with an Altar-tomb. The tomb has the effigy of Isabel with Sir Bertram's own image kneeling at her feet in grief. Over the inner doorway of the vestibule leading to the chapel are the remains of a Latin inscription "My tears have been my food day and night."

Some say Warkworth Castle's Grey Lady is Sir Bertram's Isabel, trying to get her message of forgiveness to him. Others say the inconsolable ghost of Sir Bertram of Bothal still haunts the castle and the Hermitage.

Warkworth castle has a chilly atmosphere and sensitive dogs have been known to show reluctance to enter its formidable walls. Children, it is said, become strangely quiet and contemplative when they enter the dark exterior, seeming to fall under the castle's strange spell.

The ghost of a young man has also been seen running along the walls of the castle.

The Viking Ghost of Tynemouth Castle

The castle and priory at Tynemouth in Northumberland stands proudly at the mouth of the river Tyne, keeping watch over the North Sea. The Priory, a burial place for early Northumbrian kings was founded in 617, then after being destroyed by the Danish invasions, was rebuilt in 1090. Tynemouth Castle was built in the 14th century as a coastal defence.

The ruins of Tynemouth Priory are said to be haunted by the ghost of a Viking called Olaf. Some say that his life was saved by the kind Monks of the Priory who nursed him back to health when he was badly wounded in a raid of the area. According to legends he stayed on and joined their community. The Vikings returned and during another raid, Olaf's brother was killed in the fighting. Olaf was struck with grief and died not long afterwards while praying in the Chapel. His ghost can sometimes be seen wandering through the priority or standing, looking wistfully out over the sea towards his homeland.

The Green Lady of Comlongon Castle, Dumfries, Scotland

Crossing the Border into Scotland now and apparently, below the watchtower of Comlongon Castle in Dumfries, there is a patch of grass that refuses to grow. This is the spot where it is said Lady Marion Carruthers landed after having thrown herself off the tower.

Her sobbing ghost wanders sadly through the rooms and corridors of the castle.

Lady Marion had inherited a huge estate including Mouswald Castle from her father. Neighbouring families, the Douglas's and the Maxwells' had their eye on her lands and prior to his death, Lady Marion's father had given his consent for Marion to marry Sir James Douglas.

Mouswald Castle, however, was invaded by the Maxwells and Lady Marion fled to her uncle at Comlongon Castle near Gretna. She was desperate to escape the intended marriage and gave her uncle half of her dowry. Her intended, Sir James Douglas, was not going to give up that easily. Her late father had given consent to the marriage and he sued for the Estate stating that he had prior rights through the marriage contract. Sir James won the case. Lady Marion was ordered not to return home until her marriage was settled.

She could not escape her forthcoming marriage in life and therefore, according to some stories, on the 25th September

1570 she chose to escape her Fate by throwing herself off the Lookout Tower at Comlongon Castle, to her death.

Some could not believe this was suicide and blamed Sir James Douglas' men of throwing herself off the top of the Castle so Sir James would inherit all her lands without having to marry the reluctant bride.

As well as the spot where she threw herself to her death being marked by the fact that no grass will grow in this area, Lady Marion's ghostly figure dressed in green has been seen wandering through the castle, crying. Her favourite haunting place is the suite of the rooms known as the Carruthers Suite.

Often, when she appears, there is a smell of apples and this ghost, so it is said, also has a habit of moving jewellery from one room to another. Some say that because she had taken her own life, she was not given a Christian burial and her ghost wanders in search of her proper resting place.

Haunted Castles in the UK

The picturesque Eilean Donan Castle is one of the most photographed castles in Scotland. Sitting on a rocky islet where three lochs meet, the castle has a fascinating history. In the early 1300s Randolph, earl of Moray, had 50 men executed at Eilean Donan and ordered their heads to be spiked on the castle walls. But it is the ghost of a Spanish soldier who was killed during a siege in the early 1700s that is said to haunt the castle. Also, one of its bedrooms is haunted by the ghost of a lady.

In Dingwall, Scotland stands the 12th Century Tulloch Castle which as well as being an impressive fortress, is now a hotel with its magnificent hallways, original fireplaces and ceilings and a 250 year old panelled Great Hall.

Room eight in particular is said to be the most haunted. The forlorn ghost of a lady dressed in green wanders through the building and it is said she died falling down the staircase. Others believe the Green Lady might be the ghost of Elizabeth Davidson. – Her portrait can be seen hanging in the Great Hall. One male guest reported to have woken up one night to find two female ghosts sitting on his chest, apparently trying to suffocate him!

Rattling door handles, the loud ticking of a clock and other things that have gone bump in the night have kept residents awake at night while ghostly figures have been seen standing at the foot of beds.

Castles all over the UK are said to be haunted and many hold regular Ghost Hunts.

At Warwick Castle, for instance, visitors are invited to join overnight ghost hunts. This magnificent Castle in England is reputed to be haunted by the restless spirit of Sir Fulke Greville who was murdered at the castle by his manservant. There are many recorded ghost sightings at Warwick Castle, including some captured on security camera. Cleaners and security personnel have reported eerie happenings and encounters with spirit beings. So it's hardly surprising that the castle often conducts ghost hunts for those who dare brave its haunted rooms and empty corridors on dark, eerie nights.

Many paranormal events have taken place in Gwyrch Castle in Wales which is haunted by a White Lady, a Red Lady and a Butler, among others. Some stories tell of how, after a séance at the castle, a solid oak door was ripped off its hinges. Although now in a dilapidated state of repair, this has been said to be one of the most haunted castles in Wales.

There have been many eerie encounters and ghostly tales connected with Windsor, one of the most well-known castles in the UK. Henry VIII's dragging footsteps can be heard in the deanery cloisters while it is said that Elizabeth I haunts the royal library. Some have seen the sad face of mad King George peering out of a window while Charles I haunts a Canon's house in the Castle precincts.

The ghost of a young Grenadier Guard who shot himself while on duty at Windsor Castle haunts the Long Walk. The kitchen of one of the buildings in the castle grounds is haunted by a man leading a horse, while ghostly footsteps can be heard on many of the Castle's staircases.

Throughout the UK stand scores of grand and many now sadly ruined castles. And whether visiting some of the more majestic buildings or one of the more desolate places, each and every one will have its own ghostly tale or two.

Part 1 Chapter 2

Haunted Houses and Inns you can Experience for Yourself

All Houses and Inns mentioned in the following ghostly tales are open to the public.

Ghostly Entities of Lydiard House, Wiltshire

The haunted Lydiard House in Wiltshire, ancestral home of the Viscounts Bolingbroke is open to the public all year round. Successive generations of Oliver St John's family have made changes to the house through the centuries and a number of ghosts are said to haunt the area. Sir John St John's life in the late 1500s was full of tragedy. He lost three of his sons to the English Civil War.

Sir John St John's ghost is regularly seen leaning against the fireplace in the Morning Room of Lydiard House. The appearance of his ghost is said to follow a marked drop in temperature and a sickly sweet fragrance which some people have described as smelling like sweet tobacco. Those who have seen him describe him as a "solid figure" and if it wasn't for his 17th century clothing, he could easily be mistaken for a living person. His spirit has also been seen strolling around the grounds of the house.

Also dating back to the Civil War a little drummer boy has been seen walking in the night tapping on his drum although no beat has ever been heard. The avenue leading up to the house is haunted by a phantom coach and horses while a lady in white also drifts across the grounds. The White Lady has also been seen on the staircase inside the house. Some think she might be the ghost of Lady Blunt because the apparition is most commonly seen on the 30th October, the anniversary of her fiancé's murder.

The church within the grounds is said to be haunted by a number of ghosts. One of the most eerie is a grey, hooded figure whose presence brings a feeling of chilly malevolence. Even when no ghosts have manifested, there have been chilling sounds heard in the church and these include a woman sobbing pitifully and solemn organ music coming from inside the empty building.

Ghostly Loseley House, Surrey

Photograph: Wikimedia commons

Among other spiritual entities, two female ghosts are believed to haunt the Elizabethan mansion, Loseley House in Surrey. These ghosts look very similar but it is the feeling people get when they appear that distinguishes one from the other. These spirit presences are believed to have lived in the 18th century and one is known as the Pleasant Lady and the other, the Unpleasant Lady.

From their names it is obvious how people feel when they witness one of these ghostly figures. When the Pleasant Lady appears, people feel a sense of calm and get a sense that the ghost is charming and friendly. When the Unpleasant Lady visits, people have reported feeling an intense mood of anger, hostility and hatred in the room.

It is even said that an American visitor in the 1930s was so spooked by the appearance of the Unpleasant Lady that he ran out of the house and refused to go back inside. He waited, still overcome with terror, while someone else packed all his things for him and he swiftly left refusing to ever return.

One of Loseley's more pleasant ghosts is a smiling lady dressed in Victorian clothes. The present owner who saw the ghostly figure later found a portrait of her in the attic.

Owned by the More-Molyneux family since the sixteenth century, Loseley House has had many famous guests including Queen Elizabeth I, King James I, Queen Anne and Queen Mary. The home also has associations with the famous poet John Donne who secretly married the grand-daughter of Sir William More who first began the building-work of Loseley House. (See my book "From His Mistress.")

Visitors, servants and guests of Loseley House have sensed an atmosphere of intense evil at times within the house and many ghostly sightings have been reported. The eerie screams that were heard coming from one room, are said to have resounded through the whole mansion.

A regular ghostly figure is the Woman in Brown who has been seen standing at the bottom of the stairs. According to rumour, this ghostly figure is the second wife of one of the owners of the house who wished her step-son dead so her own son would inherit the estate. Some say she had the boy's legs cut off and he bled to death although there is mention of a painting of a woman with a legless boy sitting on her lap that was painted over by another artist. Other tales suggest the Lady in Brown drowned her step-son in the moat that was once connected to the cellars by a secret passage.

When her husband found out what she had done, he locked her in a room, so it is said, keeping her there for the rest of her life. This is the room from where, at the same time every year, horrific screams are heard, resounding around the whole house.

At the start of the 20th century, Loseley House was rented by a couple who did a lot of entertaining. After having arranged a large dinner party, they hired a waiter to serve the meals. It was a stormy night so the waiter and many of the guests stayed over. The next morning, the housekeeper asked the waiter if he had slept well. He told her that a fine-clothed gentleman had passed through his room several times during the night and he had got the impression the gentleman didn't want him sleeping there. None of the guests had been dressed in the formal style of clothing he described.

On another occasion, the couple who were renting the magnificent house left their young daughters in one of the bedrooms one night, while they were entertaining guests. The girls told their parents they would be okay on their own because an old lady dressed in grey often came to look after them. They frequently saw this elderly woman and looked forward to her visits. She would come into the playroom and sit and smile at them, as if she was taking care of the children.

It is thought that the girls may have felt she was a living nanny but when they were told they were the only ones who could see her, they realised there was something spooky about her and they stopped talking about the woman in grey.

There are numerous documented cases of dogs and other animals refusing to enter an area that is said to be haunted. Loseley is one of them. Dogs act strangely in the spot where the ghostly gentleman described above was seen. One dog that was brought into the house refused, in fear to go any further when it reached that spot. Another was with his owner who was on a tour of the house. The owner thought the dog was still following him and when the tour was over he turned to call his dog but he wasn't there. They found his pet later, crouched and whimpering in fear in the same place the other dog had also frozen.

Paranormal activity at Gunsgreen House, Eyemouth

The elegant Gunsgreen House, was built by a gentleman of the fishing town of Eyemouth, John Nisbet, who had a secret life as a smuggler. The house which has a long history has now been restored to its former glory and is open to the public.

We visited this interesting building a few years ago. Designed by one of the most famous architects of the day, John Adam, the house has many unusual features which were the special requirements of its owner. The cellar, for instance, leads straight to the sea where smuggled goods including tobacco, brandy and tea were received. Behind panels in upstairs rooms are shoots where smuggled goods can be quickly 'disposed of.' The goods would fall down the shoots into the cellar.

Visitors to Gunsgreen House have reported various unexplained paranormal activity, including fans being switched on and off and carpets being rolled back. People have had powerful feelings of being watched while walking around the cellar and through the bedrooms and staff have reported hearing strange noises and feeling uneasy in certain rooms.

One visitor reported having felt something jump on her back and shout in her ear while others have seen a woman dressed in a long grey dress wandering around the rooms on the ground floor.

The Smelly Ghost of Dumfries House

After being saved from the auctioneer's hammer at the very last minute by Prince Charles, the magnificent Dumfries House has been reformed to its former glory and is now open to the public. Built in the mid 1700s for the 5th Earl of Dumfries, the House has been described as an 18th century time-capsule with most of its 600 pieces of furniture remaining in situ as they were designed and intended for the house. It is well worth taking a tour of the house if ever you are in this area.

As for 250 years the main rooms of Dumfries House and their contents have remained virtually unchanged and during those years the house has seen a lot of history. It isn't just a privilege to visit Dumfries House but visitors feel as if they are taking a step back in time. And what is time? A good answer comes in the words of Tim Lebbon "Time has ghosts. That's what time is: the ghost of every instant passed, haunting the potential of every moment to come."

Guides who show visitors around the magnificent Dumfries House will not mention ghosts. This is not a ghost tour and whereas many houses, hotels and castles have jumped on the paranormal bandwagon Dumfries House attracts tourists for its fascinating history and amazing contents.

But there is talk of a bizarre ghost of Dumfries House which is more an 'essence' or a 'smell'. It isn't a pleasant smell and does not confine itself to any particular room. Apparently this ghost can be sensed anywhere at any time during the day or night. Perhaps it will reveal itself on one of your visits!

Haunted Inns

Haunted Happenings at Jamaica Inn, Cornwall

We could not visit Cornwall as we did some years ago with our family and not visit the Jamaica Inn. – High on Bodmin Moor stands the Jamaica Inn of Daphne Du Maurier fame. This 250 year old inn or old coaching house is one of Cornwall's most famous smuggling inns. Alongside the inn is a Smugglers Museum boasting the finest collection of smuggling artefacts in the country.

As well as enjoying a delicious meal, visitors might stay at the inn, join one of its ghost-hunts or wander through the museum and soak up its eerie atmosphere.

Photo: K Allen.

In its past, many a weary traveller must have felt a moment's relief to glimpse the coaching house, a welcome shelter from the wild and rugged landscape. But the inn's weather-worn walls also provided a perfect hiding place for smuggled goods and inspiration for many tales of smuggling including Daphne Du Maurier's novel of the same name.

It is said that on a dark, cold and eerie night the writer stayed at the inn and the spooky atmosphere and legendary history of the inn inspired her to write her novel about smuggling on the Cornish coast. Once a haunt for smugglers, Jamaica inn now has a reputation for regular haunted happenings.

People have reported hearing the sound of horses' hooves and the wheels of coaches being pulled along the rough cobbles of the courtyard. Footsteps have been heard wandering the corridors of the inn at night when there was no-one there and a tall man, dressed in a tricorne hat and coat has been seen walking through solid doors. A previous manager of the inn told of having heard conversations in a different language.

Legend has it that a long time ago a traveller was drinking a tankard of ale at the bar when he was called outside. He left his half-finished tankard on the bar as he stepped out into the night and this was the last time he was seen alive. For the next day his body was found on the bleak moor. How he was killed and who killed him remains a mystery but those who have heard footsteps walking along the passage to the bar believe it is the dead man's ghost returning to finish his drink.

In the early 1900s there was a lot of conjecture about the strange man who had been seen by many people sitting motionless on the wall outside the inn. He made no acknowledgement of seeing anyone around him and his appearance is said to be uncannily like the man who was murdered on Bodmin Moor.

Ghostly Reflections at Edenhall Country Hotel, Penrith

Originally called Woodbine Cottage, the oldest parts of Edenhall Hotel in Penrith, Cumbria, date back to the mid-17th century. Many ghosts haunt the rooms and corridors of the hotel but one that is seen most often is the lady in room 4 (originally room 25). Both guests and staff have reported seeing a female ghost sitting on the edge of the bed. Some guests saw her reflection through the mirror in the bathroom while they were using the bath tub. Other tales speak of guests seeing the ghostly woman materialising out of the mirror while they were taking a bath.

The hotel also used to have a number of mirrors above the bar but these had to be removed after guests and staff started complaining about seeing spooky shadows and apparitions in the mirrors. Removing mirrors did not however remove the ghosts and an old woman is often seen walking towards a chair in the corner of the bar to sit down and watch the comings and goings at Edenhall Hotel.

The Pining Ghost at Lord Crewe Hotel, Blanchland, Northumberland

The beautiful, medieval village of Blanchland on the Northumberland/Durham border grew out of the foundation of an Abbey in 1165. Properties belonging to the abbey were sold off in 1532 after King Henry VIII dissolved monasteries. After several ownerships, Blanchland was bought in the 18th century by the Bishop of Durham, Nathaniel Lord Crewe. The Lord Crewe's Charity, (provided for by a legacy from his Will), still owns Blanchland Estate today. Present visitors to this picturesque village could almost feel they were stepping back in time and visitors from the past also frequently visit the present.

The most haunted building in this remote settlement is said to be the Lord Crewe Arms which was originally the Abbot's Lodgings built in 1165. Charming and idyllic, the hotel retains its medieval atmosphere while another residue of medieval times is its resident ghost, Dorothy Forster. Dorothy's brother, Tom Forster was an MP who plotted the 1715 Jacobite rebellion although he had little if any experience of military matters. He marched his troops about the country with no great effect until he surrendered without a fight at Preston. When his sister, Dorothy, heard he had been taken to London to be tried for treason, she persuaded the village Blacksmith to take her to the capital on his horse. They rode the hundreds of miles to London and using bribes and trickery, Dorothy succeeded in rescuing her brother. They returned to the family property where Tom was hidden in a priest-hole until he could be spirited away to France, where he would be safe.

Visitors can still see the priest-hole in the giant fireplace in the Hilyard room of the Inn, a room which was once used for smoking and curing meat. Behind the chimney is the hiding hole used by catholic priests and where Tom had also hidden. The plan was that he would go to France and the siblings would get in touch with each other once things had calmed down in England but Tom was never able to return. His sister was never the same after he left the country, so upset was she by their separation. When he died abroad and she heard of his death she was so distraught that according to their story, she pined away from her loss. Dorothy's ghost still haunts the Lord Crewe Arms as her spirit yearns to be reunited with her brother. Visitors report seeing shadows and feeling suddenly chilly when she visits.

Is the Skirrid Inn, Abergavenny the Scariest Place Ever?

The oldest and perhaps the most haunted pub in Wales, Skirrid Inn, is mentioned in records as far back as 1110. Named after Skirrid Mountain by which it stands, the mountain has its own legends. Apparently at the time of Jesus' crucifixion the mountain cracked in two.

If only buildings could talk, think of the history this Inn has seen: wars, rebellions, religious conflict and witchcraft. Some say the brutal judge George Jeffreys (who was appointed by James II to try rebels) began his career at the Skirrid Inn although there is no evidence to prove this. Jeffrey's sentenced 200 to hanging in his career and he had 800 rebels transported to the West Indies.

Tales linked to the Skirrid Inn tell of 180 hangings having taken place between the 12th and 17th Centuries from a beam on the staircase. The beam
supposedly still has marks made by the rope. The first floor of the Inn is thought to have once been a court room, with a cell where prisoners would have spent their last night before their execution.

Doors being slammed, loud footsteps, and hushed unexplainable voices have been heard by guests staying at the Inn which has appeared in the TV show "Most Haunted" and in "Extreme Ghost Stories." Some say Skirrid Inn is one of the scariest places they've ever visited. Faces have been seen at the windows, objects will fly across rooms apparently of their own volition and other things mysteriously disappear and turn up again weeks later. Other eerie happenings include guests waking to an icy cold room with a feeling of being watched.

Hangman's Rope, Skirrid Inn.
Photo: P. Halling

Response from ghost-hunting guests staying at the inn include "... the spooks didn't disappoint!" and "had some really good experiences and got some great footage of orbs." "Got loads of orbs in pictures we took and when we got into bed, bags we had at the far end of the room began to rustle as soon as we switched the lights off."

The Golden Fleece Pub in York

The Golden Fleece is one of the oldest Coaching Inns in York although it wasn't always an Inn. Between 1503 and 1557 it was owned by the Merchant Adventurers. A Merchant was someone who traded in bulky goods such as wool or wood as opposed to a Mercer or Grocer who traded in dry goods and foodstuff. The Golden Fleece's Merchants traded in fleece and wool. Later the Inn became a coaching station for travellers coming from and travelling between York, Manchester and Liverpool. It boasted of having excellent beds, a comfortable sitting room and excellent stables and coach houses. The Inn was popularly used by jurymen, witnesses and others having business at the Law Courts.

Anyone staying at the Golden Fleece should be aware of the possibility of having the company, whether invited or not, of other unworldly residents. Many visitors mention the unusual amount of orbs in photographs they have taken inside the building.

A ghostly lady wanders the meandering corridors and floats above the staircases. Ghostly figures have been seen moving furniture while clothes have been taken off rails in the wardrobes and thrown onto the floor. Bed clothes have been pulled off the beds.

Included in the ghosts that haunt this wooden-framed building is a WWII Canadian airman, Geoff Monroe. It is said that after a heavy drinking session, he fell out of a window, to his death on the pavement below. Guests staying in 'his' room have reported seeing a figure in full uniform standing over them while they were lying, terrified, in bed. They had been woken by his cold touch.

A ghostly figure was also witnessed by a group of people, during a ghost hunt in 2002. Dressed in late 17th century clothes, the ghost appeared from out of a wall and sauntered across the corridor to the Shambles bar. As he crossed the corridor the ghost turned to look directly at the utterly amazed (and some terrified) ghost hunters before heading for the bar.

With its uneven floors and weird angles of floors and ceilings, the pub is said to have no foundations. The Golden Fleece has a reputation of being the most haunted pub in the county.

The Schooner Hotel, Alnmouth

With over 3,000 reported sightings and boasting 60 individual ghostly spirits, ghost-hunters stand a high chance of experiencing paranormal activity at the Schooner Hotel in Alnmouth. Regular ghost hunts are held by the Hotel's resident medium and it also has a Facebook page to report the latest supernatural phenomenon going on within its walls.

(dining room of this haunted hotel, photo: C West)

This 17th century Coaching Inn is reputed to have had many notable guests including Charles Dickens, King George III and Douglas Bader. Like Eyemouth further up the coast (see Paranormal Activity at Gunsgeen House in part (i) of this book), Alnmouth was also known to be a haven for smugglers. And like Gunsgreen House, the hotel had a secret tunnel used for smuggling, running from the cellar to the sea. Strange lights and eerie figures have been seen in the cellar.

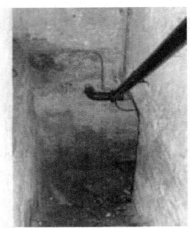
photo: C West
Schooner Hotel

There have been ghostly sightings and/or paranormal activity experienced in every room of the Schooner Hotel with room 28 apparently being the most haunted. This is said to be the site of a family massacre as well as numerous suicides. The family were from France and according to legends about the hotel, they were murdered by a gypsy who then stole all their belongings. Guests have reported a feeling of overwhelming terror and some have refused to stay in this room.

Two members of the Hotel staff reported seeing and hearing a large dark figure flying out of room 20 to bang straight into the fire doors opposite. It did not go through the doors but turned instead to come bounding towards them as they stood in the corridor. Both members of staff ran, thinking the hotel was being burgled but when the corridor was checked, there was no evidence of anyone having been there.

Photo: C West
Schooner Hotel

Just talking with a guest who took part in a ghost hunt at the Schooner Hotel makes the hair stand the back of the neck. Other worldly presences could be felt in almost every part of the building. Could it be that ghostly presences have drawn energy from those who visit the hotel expecting and most of the time meeting with some form of spiritual encounter? Could the ghosts be feeding off this immense interest (energy) which has made the hotel famous for its hauntings and could this make supernatural activity grow stronger?

A huge amount of paranormal activity has been experienced in rooms 16 and 17 with ghostly figures having been seen standing by beds and in the corridor just outside these rooms. The blocked-off doorway which was discovered in between these two rooms is believed to have something to do with these supernatural happenings.

The Schooner Hotel has been the subject of many paranormal investigations which have confirmed that ghosts haunt the hotel. Eager and experienced ghost-hunters who spent the night at the hotel told me it is the most haunted and eerie place they've ever visited. Dare you experience this for yourself? A visit to the Schooner Hotel is only a booking away!

The Ghosts of Kirkstone Pass, Cumbria

Photo: J Firth

The third highest Inn in England in the beautiful setting of the Lake District, the Kirkstone Inn is close to the summit of the Kirkstone Pass. The Inn is named after the large stone standing close by, the Kirk Stone. In the 1800s the building was used as a coaching house and with a variety of uses including a garage in the 1950s, it is now a country Inn which has been the scene of some scary supernatural activity.

Visitors have described the Inn in this remote location as feeling eerie, oppressive, isolated and yet being also fascinating. People who worked (and lived) at the Inn report having heard strange sounds, witnessed ghostly figures and are quite firm in their belief that the building is haunted. One family reported that on their visit, their dog refused to set foot inside the eerie building.

It is thought that there was once an ancient monastery dating back to the 15th century in the place where the Kirkstone Inn now stands. And throughout the Inn's long history there have been many supernatural occurrences. Tourists and those working in the surrounding area have reported seeing ghostly apparitions which are thought to be the spirits of weary travellers who died whilst walking in this remote area.

A tree, close to the Inn, is where a woman was hanged for having murdered her young child. The woman's ghost is said to linger close to the tree, appropriately called the Hangman's Tree!

A young boy who was killed by a coach just outside the Inn is said to haunt the place whilst poltergeist activity within the Inn has been blamed on the ghost of a hiker who once worked there.

One traveller whose ghost now haunts Kirkstone Inn was a young girl from Patterdale called Ruth Ray. As the story goes, she and her young daughter were on their way to visit her sick father when the weather changed abruptly as it so often does in the Lake district. Snow began to fall and before too long, heavy snowflakes made it impossible for anyone to see very far. Ruth could easily have lost her bearings and could have been walking in any direction however it seems she managed to stick with the familiar path because when she didn't return home, her husband set off to search for her, taking the road he knew she would have used. Sadly, he eventually found her frozen, lifeless body. She had wrapped her baby snugly and thanks to her thoughtfulness although she could not save her own life, her child survived. Ruth's ghost haunts Kirkstone Pass Inn when the weather is particularly bad and some say her spirit warns walkers of the dangers of the area in times of inclement weather.

Captured on film, the ghost of a coachman dressed in 17th century attire, appeared mysteriously on a photograph that was taken in front of the Inn in 1993. It is said that the ghost was the great, great grandfather of the family who were photographed and apparently it followed them home and now lives with them!

Skinburness Hotel, Silloth, Cumbria

(Skinburness Hotel Vintage Postcard)

Standing one mile north of Silloth, the once grand and now derelict Skinburness Hotel opened as a hotel in the late 19th century. The building has been a family home, a hydro spa and was once used by the government as part of the Carlisle State Management Scheme between 1916 and 1971. Visitors who stayed at the Hotel speak of it fondly. Staff were friendly, rooms spacious and food was good. Some say the place had a special feel about it with its maze of rooms and unique layout, others now feel the ruins have a creepy and ominous atmosphere.

The original building was designed by local architect Charles Ferguson in 1878 and up until 2006 it was operating as a hotel. Planning permission was granted for its demolition and the construction of a nursing home but this expired in 2013 and the ruins of this once magnificent building still stand.

There is a distinct aura of sadness about the ruins now while some feel it is not only eerie but there is something sinister that lingers within the deserted rooms and corridors. A woman who recently passed it by felt it was an 'awful place' that gave off really bad vibes. She got the worst feeling she has ever had about a building and wanted to get as far away from it as she could as quickly as possible!

(Skinburness Hotel, Silloth vintage postcards)

Above photographs Skinburness hotel in its prime

The hotel has been standing derelict since 2006 when the owners, Adrian and Vanessa Moore who had owned the hotel for little more than a year were declared bankrupt and everything that could be auctioned off was sold. It is likely to be soon demolished. The couple had put a lot of money and effort into restoring the building including obtaining a civil licence in order to hold weddings at the hotel. Business had been good with travel companies keeping the hotel busy with a steady stream of coach parties.

Christmas 2005 was a good year for the hotel but it was followed by a poor winter which caused visitors to cancel without any notice. By August 2006 the owners admitted to having financial problems due to a lack of pre-booked coach trade and increasing staff costs. Trading ceased in September.

A team of local ghost-hunters returned from a visit one night with some eerie photographs and videos. The three experienced ghost-hunters all reported feeling as if they were being watched and as if their presence was resented. On asking for a sign of someone being there, captured on video, a door was slammed shut on one occasion while there were also sounds of objects being moved around the photographer on other videos, although no-one was there.

Thousands of people will have walked through the doors of the building during the course of its lifetime which now sadly will soon come to an end. Impressions of those visiting the place veer between both ends of the scales. It is almost as if the derelict building chooses whether it likes or dislikes its visitors and teases them with eerily spooky sensations and poltergeist activity or it welcomes their presence and gives off a warm, more embracing aura.

Skinburness hotel, photos: C West 2013

So, it has been described as having a warm, family atmosphere and also as being sinister and uncannily disconcerting. If buildings had feelings, comparing photographs of what this building once was to what it is now, one can almost understand the different impressions given off by these old walls depending on its mood of the moment!

The building was sold to its new owners for £450,000 and locals hoped it would be kept as a hotel. However there have also been rumours that the building is likely to be knocked down. Prince Charles professed his support for the Save the Skinburness Group's campaign for the building to stay faithful to its prior use.

Ghostly Ruins of Kirklinton Hall, Cumbria

(Kirklinton Hall Open Day April 2013)

Whereas the Fate of the ruins of Skinburness Hotel remains uncertain, the ruins of what was once the grand Kirklinton Hall have a more optimistic outlook as its new owners intend to restore the building to its former glory.

The history of the house can be traced back to the 1660s when it was built from the stone of a nearby castle for Edmund Appleby. From its origins as a bleak Border fortress, in Victorian times, the building was renovated and almost doubled in size. In 1875 it was extended for the Kirklinton-Saul family. During the war it was taken over by the RAF. In the 1960s the building was used as a gangsters' gambling den with a rather dubious reputation: an enterprise which supposedly the Kray twins had an interest in. It is also said it was once a hotel but after a destructive fire in the 1970s the building has stood derelict until now when it is being restored to its former beauty.

Some people who have visited the place, drawn by the fascination of these incredible ruins and the romantic atmosphere reported hearing scary noises that encouraged them to leave the place quicker than intended. Is Kirklinton Hall haunted? Many locals think so and permission has been granted by the owners for public ghost hunt events to be arranged at the Hall.

The Ghost of the Bell Inn, Essex

Thorp-le-Soken Vintage postcard prior 1945

There are few old English inns and taverns that do not boast the odd 'spirit' or two and this tale involves the Bell Inn in Thorpe-le-Soken in Essex. Guests would report seeing and hearing strange noises in one of the upstairs bedrooms. Chairs would be shifted around and even a wardrobe was seen to move from one side of the room to another. On another occasion, a guest reported having been lying in the four-poster bed when it began to float in the air.

In the 1970s the manager of the Bell Inn, Mr Eaton confirmed that he had received many reports of paranormal happenings at the hotel and in fact his mother had seen the phantom of a female, shadowy figure at the foot of her bed. She lay frozen with fear, watching, as the phantom glided slowly towards the door and then seemed to 'slide right through it.'

It is customary to look behind such happenings, to find a reason and this was not difficult. Local legend spoke of this as being the unhappy spirit of Kitty Canham who lived in the early 1700s.

Catherine Canham had wed the much older Rev Alexander Henry Gough and apparently because of his violent temper, it was not a happy marriage. Eventually, having suffered enough at her husband's hands and after the sad death of their child, Kitty took herself off to enjoy the thrills of London. Here she became the talk of high-society, mixing with all the latter day drop-outs and 18th century jet setters. Inevitably, she met someone quite unlike her older, domineering husband and romance developed. A strong attraction drew her to the handsome and wealthy, Lord Dalmeny, eldest son of the Earl of Rosebery.

Lord Dalmeny (John Primrose) fell in love with the vicar's wife and not being aware that she was married already, asked her to be his bride. She readily agreed. After the couple were married, they travelled all over Europe; a life of parties and social gathering which lasted three years. In 1752, in the Italian city of Verona (home of Romeo and Juliet) Kitty fell sick and on her deathbed, she confessed her sin of already being wed to the vicar of Thorpe. She also asked for her body to be buried in England.

After she died, the distraught Lord Dalmeny had her body embalmed in spirit, sealed in a lead coffin and packed in a heavy wooden chest. His intention was to transport it by a small boat, to England, land at Harwick and to carry the coffin through the back lanes to Thorpe, where it could be buried secretly at the Vicarage. However, they came upon an awful storm and the ship was blown off course to end up at the River Colne.

In those days, smuggling was not unusual and Custom and Excise officers spotted the large chest aboard the storm-damaged ship and questioned Lord Dalmenly about its contents. Not satisfied with his explanations, one of the Excise officers plunged a long steel spike into the side of the chest, swamping the deck with raw spirit. Inside, they found the corpse of a young and beautiful woman and Lord Dalmeny was taken into custody on suspicion of murder. It was then that he confessed the true identity of the corpse.

Rev Alexander Gough was contacted by the authorities and rushed to Colchester. On coming face to face with his rival in love, Lord Dalmeny, he immediately challenged the young man to a duel but on seeing the body of his wife, he realised how devoted the young man had been and his heart softened. The two men forgot their differences and actually became good friends. They arranged a special funeral and in a coffin adorned with silver name plate and nails, the wife with two husbands was buried in Thorpe churchyard to rest in peace until...

During the mid-1800's, extensive restoration work was carried out to the church and several graves were destroyed in the process. From that time onwards, weird, spooky and unexplained 'happenings' began at the Bell Inn. Most strangely too, a fire that ravaged the building failed to damage a painting of Kitty that hung on the wall!

For in 1999 a devastating fire destroyed all the roof of the Inn and left the cottages attached badly damaged but Kitty's painting remained intact. All the more reason for people to believe that it was Kitty to blame for the paranormal activity in the Inn. It took two-and-a-half years for the building to be renovated to its present state under the watchful eye of the English Heritage Trust. During the renovation, a huge fireplace which had been previously bricked up was discovered.

Prior to the fire, the Greens lived in the adjacent cottage which is also said to be haunted. Previous owners of the cottage told them that their dog would not enter the dining room but would stand at the doorway and growl. The dining room and the bedroom above were next to the Bell Inn. The beams in these rooms were of heavy oak and the floorboards were worn with age. It is thought that these rooms were constructed in the early 18th century.

Although they had been told the cottage was haunted, the Greens did not experience anything overly supernatural at first. Occasionally they would return to the house to find that doors they had shut had been opened while they were away and the smoke alarm in the dining room would start bleeping for no apparent reason but they weren't unduly perturbed by this.

Then one night on going to bed, they found the underside of the quilt that had been facing the mattress was soaking wet. Yet the top was bone dry. No logical explanation could be found for this. Another time Steve Green had been handing his wife, Linda something in the living room when a huge drop of water landed on his hand. Both looked up expecting to see drips coming from the ceiling but nothing could be seen. There were no water pipes running across the ceiling and no condensation within the room either. Strangely, ghostly occurrences within the Bell Inn also involved water.

Another night at around 3 am a huge crash from downstairs woke up the family. Mr Green went down to investigate. Later his wife crept downstairs, with thumping heart, wondering where he was. She saw her husband on the kitchen floor surrounded by paint. It was everywhere and yet they could not work out how it had been spilt. The paint tin had been left tightly sealed on the floor.

One night after their son had a bad dream he came into their bed for comfort. Linda was too hot so left him sleeping in their bed while she went to her son's room. This room was above the dining room and next to the Bell Inn. Later that same night, she was woken up by the sound of a girl screaming. The screams seemed to go on and on and were piercing and intense. She ran to the window that looked out over the moonlit churchyard but could not see anything unusual. No-one else had heard the screams.

On the morning of the day of the fire which was the 28th July 1999, their four year old son was on the computer when Linda heard him shouting "Stop looking at me, you stupid lady." Linda looked out of the window expecting to see a passer-by but there was no-one around that she could see. She told her son off for calling people 'stupid.' Approaching lunchtime, she heard him shouting at the 'stupid woman' again. Linda saw no-one outside and when she asked her son who he was talking to, he replied that the stupid lady kept looking at him and pointed to a spot in front of Linda. She could see no-one in the room. Understandably, her young son became annoyed and agitated because his mother couldn't see the lady.

Throughout the day and into the evening their son, Joshua kept referring to the 'stupid lady' and as his mother tucked him into bed that night, he told her that the woman had said to "get out!" A few hours later at around 11 pm the whole family really did have to 'get out' very quickly as the Inn had caught fire. They lost their home and all their possessions in the fire.

The landlord of the Inn later told Linda that despite an entire wall of the Inn being badly burnt, the picture of Kitty Canham that had been hanging on that wall had survived intact.

(Thorpe le Soken vintage postcard prior 1945)

The story of Kitty Canham's ghost doesn't stop there. A month after the fire Linda Green went to the cottage with her sister. It still smelled of the fire and they walked sadly around the debris; her home had been completely destroyed and had lost its homely feel. Linda was told that the ghostly woman was still there, watching her. The ghost, it is said, knew Linda had been discussing her with Joshua and she was angry. Linda, at this time, was pregnant which, she felt, displeased Kitty who had lost her own child. This child was buried under the plum tree in the garden. There was a feeling the ghost who had died at the age of 32 was very, very annoyed about something.

Linda suddenly felt scared; she didn't mind sharing her home with a ghost but not a spirit that intended her or her family harm.

In the following year while still waiting for her cottage to be restored, in a conversation with her son, Joshua, he asked her, "Do you love ghosts?" His mother wondered at the strange question which was followed up with: "What about Kitty Canham? … She loves me you know!"

Linda didn't know where Joshua had heard the name Kitty Canham and his next sentence horrified her, sending icy shivers down her spine: "Why would she harm your children?" Shocked, Linda replied that she didn't think any harm would come to her children because she loved them all so much. Her son then responded with, "She would never harm us. She loves me."

He also went on to say that the woman slept in his room at night and sometimes did the housework. A number of things puzzled Linda about the conversation. No one had mentioned Kitty's name in front of Joshua. She also wondered why he had referred to himself and his brothers as 'your children' and not 'us' which would have been more natural. They were very careful not to mention Kitty or the ghostly woman after that conversation.

Thorpe-le-Soken is not only the last resting place of Kitty Canham but it is also where Royal physician Sir William Withey Gull who died in 1890 is said to be buried. He was an important figure in the world of medicine and was appointed as physician to Queen Victoria. However there was also a darker side to this man and many people speculated that he may have been Jack the Ripper.

Stephen Knight who was researching Jack the Ripper is said to have visited Gull's Grave at Thorpe-le-Soken where both he and his wife are buried. The Verger, at the time, had pointed out it was a large grave, twelve by nine feet, "Too large for two people." Some say more than two are buried there. Even stranger is there had been rumours within the community of Thorpe-le-Soken that Gull had not died when it was stated he had. The funeral had been a sham and he'd been buried late at night, several years later. If his death had been faked, could this be because there were suspicious he was linked with Jack the Ripper? Speculation continues.

Real Ghost Stories (ii) Hauntings, Postergeists and Supernatural Beings

Tales of ghosts and spirit hauntings have been a part of folklore almost since time began. People are fascinated by ghosts and even if you don't believe in them, you've probably still heard some ghostly tales that made you wonder whether just maybe there are some supernatural happenings that cannot be explained.

Ghosts come in all sorts of mysterious shapes and guises that can be categorised. Part two of this book will describe some of the many categories of ghosts and hauntings and give true examples of ghostly experiences that fall in each category.

So are you sitting comfortably? Here are some ghostly tales that will send a shiver down your spine.

Types of Ghosts

Ghost stories have always fascinated people. Tales of ghosts and spirit hauntings have been a part of folklore almost since time began and often the same questions seem to arise.

Questions such as: Are ghosts real? Why might the same apparition be often seen again and again in the same place by different people? And how is it that a photograph can show an apparition which hadn't been seen by the person taking the picture?

Hauntings seem to fall into three main categories although these are far from rigid. Firstly, there's the spirit (or ghost) that is observed but the apparition seems unaware of the presence of humans. Secondly, there is the spirit/ghost that supposedly returns to see a loved one and thirdly, there is the poltergeist - the spirit that takes delight in moving objects around.

Evidence suggests that in most ghost-sightings, the person whose apparition appeared was at that time undergoing some crisis, such as a severe illness, an accident, or death. This relationship between the crisis and the apparition led researchers to conclude that the apparition was telepathic.

It is a fact that the body contains a certain amount of static electricity and from time to time, this is released. Most people will have experienced the build-up of static on their clothes. Conditions that affect the amount of electrostatic charge building up on a person include atmospheric humidity, brushing against furniture, sitting and rising from seats, the floor material and footwear. The build-up of static electricity can reach a level which, when discharged, can give a shock.

Could electrical vibrational energy and 'spirit energy' be linked? If so, we might expect to see more ghostly sightings and paranormal activity during lightning storms.

A person dying under extreme circumstances could very well cause a release of electrical energy from the body. This electricity could become embedded in the surrounding landscape, to be replayed when conditions are right.

This example would fall under the first category of hauntings when an entity is observed but does not seem to be aware of the witness. Many people have described such sightings as being like "watching a film." They also describe a drop in temperature, and their hair rising – this possibly being the effect of static in the atmosphere.

The second category of hauntings is where a loved-one returns from the dead, usually taking on the appearance of the person they used to be when once fit and healthy. Spiritualists believe that as well as matter and spirit, there is the soul, the afterlife, deities and mediums who can link with the spirit world. So, when a person dies, their soul moves on into the spirit world and this is why their ghosts appear looking fit and well.

Many religions and cultures believe in the soul and the spirit world. Hindus, for instance, believe in reincarnation. – When a person dies, their soul moves from one body to the next. Muslims believe that the soul continues to exist after physical death. Buddhists believe in 'rebirth'; when people die, they will be 'reborn' again. Maoris, too, believe that when someone dies they will go to the spirit world and they will always be a part of the 'marae' – their traditional meeting place.

One other explanation for this second category of hauntings could be that the apparition is caused by the grief of the living person, creating a "ghost image", or a mental projection of the departed.

People who have never seen an apparition may assume that no-one can see anything that is not actually physically present but this isn't so. The visual sense is much more complex than some might imagine. For instance, people often see things vividly in their dreams, even though they're receiving no visual information through their eyes.

While awake, most people can readily see in their mind's eye anything they choose to see no matter what they're looking at, at any particular moment.

Hypnotic experiments have shown that a highly suggestible person can be hypnotised to see only the hypnotist on awakening. So even if there are others in the room, this person will be unable to see them until the hypnotist removes the suggestion.

The hypnotist can tell someone what he WILL see and what he WON'T see. Could it then be that a person in crises can send a telepathic hallucination to someone else? Likewise achieving the same effect the hypnotist reaches through giving his subject explicit instructions.

Poltergeists and Ghosts

Moving on to the last category: the poltergeist. The poltergeist is a mischievous spirit that moves objects around and is generally disruptive. These manifestations tend to centre around young people often in their early teens. It has therefore been suggested that emotional problems in youngsters might cause a release of latent energy, causing objects to move around.

While there is another explanation which is accepted by some. This one says that sometimes a soul will become trapped within our planes of existence and until it is released, perhaps through exorcism, the hauntings will continue.

This section of my book will give examples of some of the many categories of hauntings including photographs of orbs and other ghostly phenomena captured by the camera.

Firstly let's hear a true poltergeist story.

The Epworth Rectory Poltergeist

It was on the night of 2nd December 1716 just before 10 pm at the home of the Reverend Samuel Wesley when his manservant and maid settled in front of a roaring fire in their master's dining-room. Here they sat, comfortably exchanging gossip before retiring for the evening. All of a sudden their conversation was loudly interrupted by a series of loud, urgent knocks on the door. The manservant, Robert Brown, rushed to the door and opened it wide but no one was there. He checked the garden, wondering if the knockings had been a prank, before returning to his seat.

But no sooner had he sat down when the knocking came again, even more violently than before. This time the pair could also hear the sound of heavy groans. On opening the door, there was still no-one to be seen. Some time, later in the evening, the knockings and groans occurred again with the same consequences on opening the door. The spooked servants decided to ignore any subsequent knockings and quickly retired to their bedrooms.

But this wasn't the end of the eerie disturbances. Because soon after Robert Brown had settled into bed he heard a noise like a turkey gobbling close to his bed. This was followed by a sound like someone stumbling over his boots and shoes but the manservant had left his shoes downstairs. The next day the two servants described the events of the night before to another maid, Betty Massy, who laughed at their story. "What a couple of fools you are!" she told them. "I defy anything to frighten me!"

But that evening, her statement was to be challenged. For while the sceptical maid was putting a tray of freshly churned butter into the pantry, she heard frightening knockings from "all over the shelves." Forgetting her previous bravado, she dropped the butter and ran.

The manifestations continued the next evening when Molly, one of the Reverend Wesley's daughters was sitting in the dining room reading. She heard the hall door open and the sound of a silk gown rustling and trailing into the room. But when looking up, there was no-one in the room with her. The soft noises of the gown could be heard distinctly as it seemed to do a complete circle around her, move to the door, and then it went back to her and moved around her once again. Molly looked up from her book to follow the noises with her eyes but nothing could be seen.

"It signifies nothing to run away," the brave girl reasoned in her head. Because "Whatever it is, it can move faster than me." So she rose, put her book under her arm and walked out of the room.

Another time, Molly's younger sister, Hetty, heard footsteps treading up and down the stairs accompanied by a vibration that seemed to shake the foundations on which the house was standing. The girls' told their mother, Susanna Wesley. Susanna was a wise and intelligent woman who told them that she could not make any judgements about this seemingly supernatural activity until she experienced it for herself. Soon after, Hetty called her mother to come quickly to the nursery.

In one corner of the room, there came sounds that were distinctly identifiable: a baby's cradle rocking, even though there had been no cradle in the nursery for years. On witnessing this, Mrs Wesley felt that there was indeed some form of supernatural influence at work, and she decided this needed to be discussed with her husband.

The reverend Wesley's reaction was typical of a practical man in that era and indeed a man of the cloth. "I am ashamed of you," he remonstrated. "These children frighten one another but you are a woman of sense and you should know better." He wanted to hear no more of it.

That evening, at 6 pm, the reverend conducted family prayers as was usual but while he was saying a prayer, a series of loud knocks broke out from all around the room, culminating in a thunderous knock for the "Amen."

This knocking continued to accompany that same prayer every morning and evening. The prayer happened to be the prayer for the King which apparently had already caused some bitterness between the couple. Wesley's wife always refused to say "Amen," to this particular prayer as she didn't believe the Prince of Orange was King. Her husband had been angry by this and vowed he wouldn't share his bed with her until she did. It is even said that he'd walked out on her and didn't return for a year following that bitter quarrel. It is also said that John Wesley, who along with his brother Charles were the founders of the Methodist movement, was the first child to be born to the couple following the husband's return.

Returning to the eerie disturbances at Epworth Rectory and these were now at their height. The family had named the ghost "Old Jeffrey" and the vicar of the nearby village of Haxey, Mr Hoole described how he had been invited by the Reverend to come and witness the disturbances. On the evening he visited, just before 10 o'clock he was told by a servant that "Old Jeffrey" was coming. Residents of the house had now begun to recognise the signs. For, every night just before ten, at the top north-east corner of the Rectory, they would hear loud creaking noises. The knocking would then travel from overhead to the nursery. Anyone who went to the nursery would hear knocking from the next room. When they went to the next room, it resumed in the nursery. The vicar witnessed all of this and with some of the family, followed the noise to the bed where Hetty lay.

The vicar watched as the Reverend Wesley (who now seemed to acknowledge the hauntings) then commanded the spirit to come to him in his study instead of frightening young children who couldn't answer for themselves.

The next evening it is said that when he went to his study, as he opened the door, it was thrust back with such violence it almost knocked him down. Loud knockings broke out from one end of the study to the other.

On another night the Reverend and his wife retired to their room for the night when three loud knocks came from the chest by their bed. They heard another two heavy blows before a series of disturbing noises began. They took a lighted candle downstairs to investigate the sounds which were like bottles being smashed, along with eerie groans and howls. They were met at the bottom of the stairs by their agitated dog who was barking, leaping and snapping out at invisible figures.

In letters passed between members of the Wesley family on the subject of these hauntings it appears there were more strangely goings-on than was openly discussed. There have been many attempts to rationalise these disturbances. Some suggestions are: pranks of the servants, rats scampering under floorboards or one of the daughters causing the knockings and other disruptions.

The hauntings may now have ceased but the question as to what caused the phenomena remains.

As far as poltergeists go, the Wesley haunting is one of the most famous in the UK and has been described as "The second best authenticated ghost story in history."

Anonymous Ghosts

Anonymous ghosts are those sightings and hauntings by ghosts who cannot be recognised by the witness or by paranormal investigators. Many of Edinburgh's ghosts, for instance, can be related to someone who was living who perhaps died a tragic death or suffered tragedy in their lifetime.

A lone piper who walks the tunnels beneath Edinburgh Castle can be traced to a piper who was sent down to explore the tunnels when they were re-discovered hundreds of years ago. He was told to play his pipes so those above the ground would know where he was. They lost track, however, of the piper and he failed to return. His pipes, they say, can still be heard as he walks the tunnels looking for an exit.

No-one, however, can explain the appearance of a headless ghostly drummer boy and he remains anonymous. This ghost first appeared during Oliver Cromwell's attack on the castle in 1650. It is now said that the drummer boy only appears when the castle is under threat and since this has not happened for a very long time, the little drummer boy's only appearance occurs in ghostly tales of the castle.

Another anonymous soul is a phantom dog who occasionally appears in the dog's cemetery in the grounds of the castle.

Ghostly Presences

Sometimes a ghost does not have to be seen to be felt. Its presence might be sensed by someone who feels like they are being watched. At the same time they may notice a marked decrease in temperature or change in atmosphere. Evil, anger and oppression are just some of the sensations that can be associated with some known haunted places while other ghosts have a more calming, joyful influence.

There are two ghostly ladies that haunt Loseley House in Surrey, for instance, and one is recognised for the unpleasant aura around her while the other has a happier, more charming presence. Some ghosts seem capable of creating odours that were perhaps associated with them when they died.

Familial and Famous Ghosts

Familial ghosts are those who are recognised as being known to the person who sees them. This may be a husband, parent or some other relative, or a friend.

Historical Ghosts are sightings or hauntings of historical figures from the past or famous people. Associated with murders, imprisonment, death and executions, the Tower of London is believed to be one of the most haunted buildings in England. Some ghostly figures cannot be named but are often related to those who were murdered in the tower. Anne Boleyn's ghost is one of the most regularly sighted hauntings of the Tower. A sentry in 1864 fainted from shock when he saw her headless figure floating towards him.

Henry VI who was murdered just before midnight in the Wakefield Tower while he was kneeling at prayer, now haunts the Tower. On the evening of the anniversary of his murder, Henry's mournful cries can be heard until, as the clock strikes midnight, his ghost will rest for another year.

A ghost in the form of a White Lady haunts the White Tower, one of the oldest parts of the Tower of London. She has been seen standing at the window waving to a group of children in the building opposite. In May, 2013, this ghostly woman's perfume was so overpowering it made several people gag. One visitor felt someone tapping their shoulder.

One stormy night, a guard patrolling the gallery where Henry VIII's suit of armour is exhibited had the sudden sensation that someone was throwing a heavy cloak over him. He struggled to free himself and his phantom attacker pulled the garment tight around his throat. He broke free and rushed back to the guardroom to show the marks on his neck which were evidence of this ghostly attack.

Thomas's Tower was named after Thomas a'Becket. This Tower, according to legend, collapsed twice during construction, both occurring on Saint George's Day. The ghost of Becket was seen on both days when the Tower collapsed. The Tower was named after Becket who it was felt had caused the disruption as a means to appease the ghost. In 1240, a Monk reported witnessing Becket's ghost hitting the walls and in the 20th Century, sights and sounds of a ghostly Monk have been witnessed in this Tower.

Famous Ghosts: Mary, Queen of Scots

Perhaps one of the most famous ghosts for haunting a great number of different places is Mary, Queen of Scots. This suggests, even if only a few of these sightings are true, that not all spirits are trapped in the one place.

Queen Mary is said to have loathed her time at the cold and draughty Tutbury Castle in Staffordshire. She was held prisoner in the castle at least four times in her life and in death it seems, despite her dislike of the place, she chooses to haunt it. And this ghost doesn't always wait until darkness arrives before manifesting itself. In 1884, on a hot summer's day, Queen Mary's ghost was seen by a serving Marine. He described the ghost as having been making its way "quickly across the grass."

When it comes to verified ghost stories, one of her sightings in 2004 is as good as it is likely to get for she was seen by over forty members of Her Majesty's service! A figure in white looking just like Mary was standing at the top of the South Tower. When they first saw her, they thought it was a joke, believing the curator had dressed up to entertain them.

When it was later established that no-one who was alive had dressed up in a white gown, there was a distinct change in mood. Most incredible was how so many people had seen her.

Also seen by visitors, staff and archaeologists participating in a dig at the castle, Mary Queen of Scot's ghost seems to regularly visit Tutbury Castle.

Mary has also been seen on the oak wooden staircase in Talbot Hotel. - The staircase was rescued from Fotheringhay Castle, the place of Mary's execution and Mary will have used these stairs to get from her apartments to her execution in the great hall. While at Bolton Castle in Lancashire, Mary's ghost has been seen strolling around the courtyard in a black dress. Apparently the young girl who saw the ghost ran up to her thinking it was one of her family and described looking up into the face of a beautiful woman. The woman turned and walked away through a door leading to a spiral staircase but the girl later identified the sighting as being Mary when she saw a portrait of Mary Queen of Scots.

The ghost of a page boy is said to haunt Borthwick Castle where during one of her attempts to escape capture, Mary is believed to have dressed as a page boy. She was able to escape the castle in disguise and it seems her ghost continues to haunt the castle dressed in boy's clothing.

While at Stirling Castle, Mary's isn't the only ghost to haunt the building. There are two female ghosts, the Pink Lady and the Green Lady. Mary's ghost is believed to be the Pink Lady while the other is said to be one of her maids who rescued her from a fire in her room. While Mary slept, a candle had set fire to the curtains and canopy of Mary's four-poster bed and the maid who had woken the Queen in time to help her to safety now regularly haunts the building along with the ghost of Mary Queen of Scots.

Mary sought refuge at Craignethan Castle near Lanark which is also said to be a favourite haunt of hers and she has also been seen walking outside the forbidding Hermitage Castle in the Borders. In 2014 a group of Paranormal Investigators captured strange sounds outside the Castle on a video. They has an eerie feeling they were being followed and could hear footsteps behind them. Orbs were also captured on photographs of the Castle.

The Mary Queen of Scots Visitor Centre in Jedburgh was once used by her as a private home. Visitors reported having had a strange feeling while walking around, unexplained noises have been heard and they picked up some unusual scents. In 2012 a Paranormal Investigation Team were invited to the building. Spirits were 'picked up' by some members of the team but they held themselves aloof. Noises were heard in the bedroom on a digital voice recorder which hadn't been heard at the time of the investigation. An orb was picked up by a camcorder which had been left in Mary's bedroom. Orbs were also picked up on photographs in other rooms and in the banqueting hall, the team heard clicking sounds, footsteps and the ruffles of a dress.

Famous Ghosts: Dick Turpin

Is the thundering sound of hooves often heard in the dark of night around Stonnards Hill, the ghost of Dick Turpin and his horse racing back to Epping Forest after one of his thieving escapades? Many seem to think so.

The exploits of Dick Turpin, one of the most famous highwaymen of the 1700s inspired artists and writers of the Victorian period. His adventures appeared in popular magazines right up to the turn of the 19th century and a writer called W H Ainsworth penned a glowing account of the Highwayman escaping from the hands of vengeful lawmen, virtually by the skin of his teeth and riding to York to shake off his pursuers.

This story, it is said, is more fiction than fact but it inspired the Dick Turpin legend and also the ghost of Turpin and his horse, Black Bess.

Turpin was born in 1706 in Hempstead, Essex. His father was the landlord of the local inn and also a butcher. When he was old enough, his father put Dick Turpin to the butchering trade, a demanding trade that called for a considerable amount of skilled work and physical effort. The young man hated this work and started to look for an easier way to earn a living.

Eventually deciding it would be easier to steal than work, he ran away from home to settle in the densely-wooded area that is now known as Epping Forrest. At first he confined his unlawful activities to stealing sheep and killing deer; his knowledge of butchering enabling him to slaughter and joint his kills and sell them on the quiet. But this was still too much like hard work for the young man and stealing from other people was easier.

His first victims were travellers walking through the dark forest. Being threatened by a knife was enough to persuade them to hand over their few possessions. Turpin then began to raid empty dwellings in and on the outskirts of the forest, his not-so-nice-nature evident in one of his more sickening exploits when he held the hand of an elderly widow over a red-hot stove to get her to reveal where she was hiding her savings.

His career progressed to stealing horses and then expanded still further as he joined forces with like-minded scoundrels to become a highwayman, preying on stage-coaches travelling between the market towns in that area. He then began to venture up the Great North Road as far as Stevenage and round the outskirts of London to Hampstead

Heath; the landlord of the Spaniards Inn agreeing (or having been forced to agree) to supply a stable for the horses belonging to the highwaymen.

He wasn't a bright man and his exploits attracted attention from authorities. They planned to capture him and one evening, swooped on Turpin and his companion Tom King near Hampstead Heath. In the melee that followed his companion was mortally wounded. Turpin made his escape and from this point fiction began taking over from fact. The writer W. H Ainsworth gave a glowing account of Turpin's escape on his fictitious horse called Black Bess. No doubt Dick Turpin did escape on a horse but apparently it was not as furious an escape as described by the writer and some say it was the writer who also made up the name of his horse. Other tales describe how Black Bess is a horse he stole from a man at gun point.

A further series of blunders led to Dick Turpin's being apprehended and he was hanged at York in 1739 but his ghost, it is believed, lives on. There have been reports of people hearing Turpin regularly riding his black mare along the roads in the Stevenage area. While the Hampstead Heath area also seems to be a favourite haunting place for the ghostly Turpin and his horse. It is said that the thunder of hooves can be heard coming up Stonards Hill in the Loughton area as Dick Turpin's ghost races back to Epping Forest on his horse.

Many of the ghostly tales around Epping Forest feature mysterious horses, highwaymen and hanging.

Nobody has seen the phantom pair; the hauntings are related to the sound of the thunder of hooves with matching sensations of feeling icy cold and suddenly very fearful. There is no pattern to these hauntings but it is felt that Stonards Hill, just off Loughton High Road, at midnight is the most likely place to hear the thundering hooves of Dick Turpin's horse.

Animal Hauntings

Do animals have ghosts? It is thought that the answer is yes. Many pet owners, for instance, report having still felt or seen an animal they had a strong bond with after its death. These are often dogs and cats and they might sense it in its favourite place or feel it rub against their legs while passing them. There have also been ghostly tales of horses and other animal beings which suggests that animals do indeed have ghosts.

In parts of Cumbria some ghost sightings of a black dog are also tied to superstition. It is said that if the spectre of the dog is black and should it follow you, then someone who is near and dear to you will die. The ghost of a headless dog once roamed around the watershed of Belah and it is thought that the same ghostly animal terrified those travelling between Milnthorpe and Beetham villages.

A large headless dog haunts Eggholme near Kendal. In fact, Cumbria seems to be a favourite haunting place for dogs. Dog ghosts have been seen at Kirkby Lonsdale, Crossthwaite, Lyth and Kirkby Stephen. Motorists travelling the Shap fells have reported seeing the ghost of a large mastiff while old ghost stories talk of a ghostly figure of a large dog which was seen swimming across Lake Thirlmere.

Here's a spooky tale of a ghostly cat:

The Demon Cat of Killakee

Along with a demon cat, the Dower House at Killakee in Ireland has numerous poltergeists, is haunted by a pair of ghostly nuns and the spirits of two murdered men.

Supernatural activity in the Dower House has made many rational people nervous, alarmed the clergy and attracted media coverage and interest.

It wasn't long after she moved into the house in 1968, that the owner Mrs O'Brien learned about its spooky reputation. A group of builders who were working on renovations to the property started to report strange things that were happening during the night. Locked doors opened by themselves, eerie noises were heard and most scary was the appearance of a cat. At first the men were annoyed about being disturbed by the animal, but later they became alarmed when the cat would continue to appear without warning and could enter through locked doors.

When Mrs O'Brien first heard their tales she thought the men were letting the imaginations run away with them. It wasn't until she saw the creature for herself that she began to understand their fear. She described the animal as being about the size of an Airedale. She once saw it squatting in a hallway where all doors had been looked before the apparition appeared. The doors were still locked after it had vanished.

Another person who witnessed the demon cat was Tom McAssey, a painter who was helping to redecorate the house. One evening while he was working with the other men, they all became aware of how icy cold the room had suddenly become. Half an hour beforehand, the door to the room had been locked and bolted but now they saw it was standing open. Tom could see a shadowy figure standing in the darkness beyond.

At first he thought it was someone playing a joke on them. He called "Come in, I can see you." The three men heard a deep, guttural growl which was so scary they all ran away in panic, slamming the heavy door behind them. When they turned around, the door was open again and Tom described seeing "a monstrous cat with red-flecked amber eyes crouched there in the half light."

He later painted a picture of the cat exactly as he had seen it. On another occasion he saw a shadowy figure in the hall and challenged it. Tom reported that a deep voice had answered him, saying, "You cannot see me. You don't know who I am."

The owner, disturbed by what she and others were experiencing in the house decided to have it exorcised. From the summer of 1968 to early autumn there were no further visitations or supernatural activity. The house began to be used as a centre for amateur artists who wished to improve their painting skills and for displaying woodcarvings and sculpture. And all was peaceful for a few months.

Then, in the October of the same year, a group of show business people held a séance in the house. Although this was approached in a light hearted way, it came to an abrupt ending when lights went dim or went out altogether. All the switches were still in the 'on' position and other various manifestations terrified the sitters.

The séance seemed to trigger a new wave of hauntings as they began again in earnest at the start of 1970. A medium was called in and shortly before her arrival, the medium Miss St Clair saw two nuns and a tall man. While in a trance, Miss St Clair said that the two nuns called Blessed Margaret and Holy Mary were the ghosts of two blasphemous women who had helped serve at Black Masses during satanic rituals of the notorious 18th century Hell-Fire Club on Montpelier hill not far from the house.

This legend has been proved when in 1968 during alterations to the building, a grave was found containing the skeleton of a small human with a large skull. This supports the story about the members of the Hell Fire Club who were said to have tormented and then suffocated a deformed youth.

Once the rebuilding work was complete and the place redecorated, the cat visitations ceased but possible explanation lies in a local legend about Richard "Burnchapel"

Whaley who belonged to one of the richest families in the community. He was said to have revelled in the debauched rituals and one of these included burning a live black cat on at least one occasion and the worshipping of cats in place of Satan.

Today, there is a restaurant in the place where the old house once stood and on one of its walls is the painter's portrait of the eerie Black Cat of Killakee.

Phantom Dog of Dublin

South of Dublin is the district of Templeogue which was once a quiet old-fashioned village in the foothills of the mountains. Like most rural areas it had its own supply of tales and legends and several stories centred on the spot known as Pussy's Leap. Some of these tales actually formed the subject in the letters-to-the-editor pages of the old "Dublin Evening Mail" in the 1930s

One tale that came under discussion featured a ghostly black dog. An old resident of the district had experienced this sighting forty years previously and wanted to share it with other readers. Apparently at that time there was one delivery of letters in the morning and if anyone required the night letters they would have to call to the post office in Templeogue.

One moonlit winter night at about 9pm the reader was walking home with the letters, accompanied by a servant maid from Cherryfield. As they approached Pussy's Leap a black dog crossed their path. It got larger as it ran across and gradually out of sight. They also heard the sound of chains. Strangely, the maid had not seen the dog but had heard the rattling chains.

The experience had scared them as it had seemed "of a supernatural nature," and for years the reader was afraid to pass the Leap at night. The reader then spoke of a legend about a man who was killed some years ago by a runaway horse at Pussy's Leap and he remembered, as a boy, seeing a rough cross in the grass where this had occurred. The old residents and people from nearby villages would drop a stone on the cross whenever they passed. The advent of steam-rolled roads prevented people from keeping up this old custom. Even so, some folk of Dublin still talk about the large black dog which once walked this area that gave off the sound of jangling chains with every step that it took.

Dublin's Dolocher

Another ghostly animal tale from Dublin is that of the Dolocher. On a dark winter's night in the old district of Dublin, the figure of a woman was been seen flitting silently through the alleyways and passing windows. She was a fleeting dark silhouette against the lighted interiors. Then her terrified screams would shatter the silence, alarming all who were within earshot in the crowded houses around.

This was not a one-off incident. In the dark streets and alleys of old Dublin, during one terrifying winter, women who dared walk the streets alone became the subjects of some gruesome and savage attacks. These always occurred at night and gossip in the taverns spread that the attacker was a huge black pig which they called the Dolocher.

These events were linked with a notorious criminal who had been thrown into the old Black Dog Prison and who had committed suicide. He had been sentenced to death for the murder of a woman and with him cheating the gallows at the last minute in so dramatic a way it seems inevitable that rumour would run rife.

However an incident in the prison did cause much trepidation within the town. A sentry who had been on guard in the prison was found badly mauled and unconscious. When he eventually came to, he said that a huge black pig had attacked him. Not long after another sentry vanished. His gun was found behind his sentry-box with his clothes draped around it but there was no trace of the man himself. It was immediately assumed he had been devoured by the black pig.

Fearful people in the town started to avoid going out at night. Rumours began to spread and one report followed another of people having apparently encountered the huge black pig.

Were these reports genuine? It would seem they were when several more women were attacked at night. It reached a point where the slightest sound in the streets at night sent people hurrying for shelter. It became generally accepted that the black pig was the ghost of Dolocher, the criminal who had committed suicide in Black Dog Prison and now in spirit was on a rampage of vengeance. The terrible creature that roamed the alleyways at night became known as the Dolocher.

The story continues when one rainy night a blacksmith borrowed a women's cloak as he left a tavern to return home. He was suddenly attacked by someone who, mislead by the woman's cloak, had not realised it was a man. The blacksmith was quick to overpower his assailant who turned out to be the sentry from the prison who had mysteriously vanished.

He had clad himself in the skin of a large black pig.

Could all incidents, it has to be wondered, be attributed to a psychopath or were there ghosts haunting the alleyways of Dublin on those cold winter nights long ago?

Greyfriars Bobby

Still on the subject of animal ghosts and one famous dog ghost of Edinburgh even has its own web site: greyfriarsbobby.co.uk.

Now it is said that John Gray and his dog, a Skye Terrier, Bobby, were inseparable. Wherever John was, his dog Bobby would be there too. But John Gray, like many men just trying to earn a crust in the 1800s had had a hard life and his years spent out in all weathers working as a shepherd then later trudging the streets of Edinburgh at nights as a watchman or police officer took a toll on his health. He died of tuberculosis and pneumonia.

On the day John was buried, his faithful dog Bobby followed as his master's body was taken to the kirkyard. The little terrier watched every step of the proceedings as John's coffin was lowered into the grave and covered. The dog then walked to the mound and lay on it. It didn't matter how many times the keeper of the cemetery tried to chase the small dog away, Bobby always returned and every night would lie on his master's grave. Eventually the keeper accepted the dog wasn't going to go away and started to lay sacking at the graveside to make the nights more comfortable for Bobby.

The late John's faithful terrier began to attract a lot of attention and visitors would come to the Kirkyard to catch a glimpse of the dog who was also a stickler for routine. He knew for instance that the gunfire he heard at midday every day signalled lunchtime. This is when he would leave his master's grave to visit a nearby restaurant where he would be fed before returning to the churchyard.

In 1867 a new law meant that all dogs had to be licensed and any dog found in public places without a license would be destroyed. When he heard of Bobby's plight, Sir William

Chambers, the Provost of Edinburgh, paid for Bobby's license each year. This made Bobby the responsibility of the council and a collar was made for him stating its ownership of the small dog. For fourteen years Bobby captured the heart of those who lived nearby and he would always find a home that would welcome him in to give him food, warmth and shelter. Then on a cold winter's day in January 1872, Bobby passed away.

The dog could not be buried in consecrated grounds so they buried him just inside the gate, only yards from his master's grave. One year later, a statue and fountain was erected on the corner of Candlemakers Row to commemorate the faithful dog.

His ghost is still said to haunt the kirkyard. Many people report having seen the shadow of a terrier on John Gray's grave. But Bobby isn't the only ghost to haunt Greyfriars cemetery. Should visitors to the cemetery encounter the Mackenzie Poltergeist, they might leave the church yard with bruises, bites or cuts. This restless spirit is said to be George Mackenzie who was buried there in 1691. A number of deaths have occurred within the church yard itself and Greyfriars Cemetry has also featured in the television show: "The Scariest Places on Earth."

Beloved Pets Returning from the other Side

Our pets can be our constant companions for years and years and when they pass over the Rainbow Bridge, the grief can be indescribable. A beloved friend who has given unconditional love has been lost but perhaps not forever. Many people sense their pets returning to bring them comfort in their grief. When Donna's dog died at the age of 17, she jumped on her bed almost every night until she got another dog. Her dog's spirit also ran around the house and visited Donna's children at night. Donna's husband didn't believe her, thinking she was just wishing it until it happened to him.

A few mornings after Aileen's dog died, she could swear she heard his toenails on the floor downstairs early in the mornings. She sometimes could smell him too while her little girl often says she is talking to the dog in the house and when going for walks.

A few weeks after Janine's dog passed she could still feel him with her all the time. One night her bedroom door which was closed, opened wide with no breeze present and then she felt a thud on the end of the bed and there was an impression on her duvet where he used to lie.

Harriet has her two pet rats coming back to her in her dreams. She had them for three years and they were the most intelligent, loving and funny pets she'd ever had. She dreams of them at least once a week where they are still here and just roaming free.

When Claire's dog passed, her nails could still be heard as if she was walking on the laminate flooring. Once a friend knocked at the door and asked if they had a new dog. They hadn't but the neighbour said she had heard a dog barking and sniffing at the door.

Beth felt her mum's cat sitting on the edge of her bed one night after she had passed. Her own cat was hit by a car and killed and the night it happened she saw an apparition next to her bed of her cousin who had passed, holding her cat. She took that as him saying her cat was safe in his care. Also, her little boy has said a few times that since their cat passed he has dreamed about him.

Debbie had an American bulldog called Cassie. She had Addison's disease and had to be put to sleep. Debbie was with her, talking to her, telling her to be good. The vet said that her hearing would go last. Two days after Cassie died, Debbie was upstairs. They have a wooden floor in the living room. All of a sudden she heard her lead being dragged along the door. Debbie thought she was going mad but she was the only one in at the time. When Cassie went for a walk she would carry her lead in her mouth then play with it. Debbie felt so much comfort from that. Debbie has actually captured an unmistakable image of the ghost of her beloved dog running across her kitchen floor.

Real Ghost Stories – True Stories of Ghostly Sightings

Most ghost stories involve eerie activity and ghostly sightings. Some are exaggerated as the tales are shared as many people love a good ghost story and like to pass on their own imaginative version of a spooky tale. Others have been investigated seriously and the sightings classified as having been authentic ghost experiences.

Some ghosts haunt in specific ways, visiting the same place often at a specific time of the year or when the conditions are right: stormy weather, the night of a full moon, the anniversary of a death, for instance. Some bring a sense of peace when they appear. Some are helpful. Some are mischievous. Here's a tale of a mischievous spirit:

Ghosts of Northumbria - Who is Silky?

Silky is said to be the mischievous ghost who glides around the houses and countryside of Northumbria. Several tales have been told about this mysterious apparition, dressed in black silk.

Silky is believed, for instance, to haunt the woods, lanes and isolated farms of Belsay, near Morpeth. She seemed to delight in startling unsuspecting peasants, milk maids and horsemen. Silky would also wander to a lake in Belsay, to sit in a tree above the waterfall, to watch the waters below. The tree became known as 'Silky's Chair'.

A humped back bridge in Black Heddon, known locally as Silky's Bridge is said to be haunted by Silky. The ghostly Silky would be blamed for scaring the horses crossing the bridge. The original bridge has now been replaced.

Silky is also said to have haunted Denton Hall, a mansion to the west of Newcastle. The 'rustling' apparition seemed to prefer two rooms of the hall and was often seen floating down the stairs. One day, a wealthy young lady was staying at the Hall. She had attended a ball where she had fallen instantly in love with a handsome gentleman. When she returned to her room at Belsay Hall, she sat at her dressing table, dreaming of the evening's events. Suddenly she noticed an old woman dressed in a satin gown, in an antique chair by the fireplace.

Over her wrinkled face, she wore a dark hood. The old woman began to lecture the girl, telling her that "If you knew what I know and could see with my eyes, your pleasure would be less." She then told of the dangers of youth and the wicked ways of the times. The girl turned away for a moment but when she turned back to face the woman, the room was empty. All she could hear was the rustle of silk and footsteps treading to the door.

At the end of the eighteenth century, the local people of the village of Black Heddon were annoyed by the pranks of a mysterious spirit in rustling skirts. On lonely roads in the darkness, Silky would appear in front of lone horsemen, or even sit behind them on their mounts. Sometimes she would spook horses, causing them to be restless and agitated.

Who is this ghostly spirit? There has been talk that there was a witch who lived on the banks of the river at Black Heddon who was known as Silky because of her black silk dress. The bridge had also been named after her. Could the witch and the ghost be related?

While according to another story, a maid in one of the rooms at a house at Black Heddon was terrified one day when a ceiling suddenly crashed to the floor. She fled from the house but when the family inspected the damage, they found that it had brought down a bundle which turned out to be a dog or calf's skin filled with gold. Silky was never seen again after this incident and it is thought that she was perhaps the owner of the gold, roaming the countryside in search of it. Now that it had been found, her search was at an end and Silky could rest in peace.

Haunted Places and Haunted Vessels

Ghost Ship by John Conroy Hutcheson
(source: Wikimedia commons)

Some places are known to be haunted. Roads, woods, caves, rivers and islands have their ghosts but hauntings can also be linked with buildings, items and vessels. The Great Eastern, a massive steam ship for instance, had a reputation of being haunted. Here's its story:

The Haunted Liner

The Great Eastern, built by the Victorian inventor and engineer, Isambard Kingdom Brunel, was probably the most advanced ship of her time. And yet it was plagued by disasters, deaths and frustrations. The ship was also believed to be haunted. Passengers and crew complained of hearing deafening and constant hammering noises that rang throughout the ship at night. Officers who worried that this might be sign of a structural defect, tried to locate the source of the noises without any success.

Almost from the start the ship earned a reputation of being haunted. When work began on the ship in 1854, almost all the work was done by hand, including the lifting and placing of 30,000 wrought-iron plates. These were hand-riveted into position and the first of the strange events that were to plague the massive vessel occurred during this process.

One day, when a riveter and his boy assistant failed to report for work, although annoyed about it, the authorities took no steps to discover why. Rumour started to spread around the shipyard that the pair had been entombed inside the double-skinned hull. This was denied by those in power and construction continued.

200 rivet gangs of 1,000 men were working long days to get the job done. The narrow space between the double hulls was so small that young boys were hired to crawl into this confined space. They were working 12-hour shifts at a time to the deafening thunder of the riveters' hammers. During the

massive ship's construction other gruesome and unfortunate accidents took the lives of young boys and other workers.

The launch of the Great Eastern was more of a fiasco than a success. Worried that they would lose control of such a huge vessel by sliding her down a ramp, Brunel arranged a system of hydraulic presses to ease her into the water. But apparently the owners' gave the go-ahead for the launch before adequate preparations were made and on November 3rd, 1857 the huge hydraulic rams began to inch the vessel down into the water. Chains were being used to hold the movement steady but the men in charge of the chains had not been briefed properly; they spun out of control. One man was killed outright and others were badly injured.

In a panic, it was decided to dispense with the chains and use the rams alone. Unfortunately, there weren't enough men for the job. The huge ship lumbered ungracefully down the skids and instead of going into the water it settled into the ground, bogged down solid in the mud. For months the ship was edged closer to the water until at high tide on 30 January 1858, the Great Eastern at last took to the water.

Due to all its past problems and a lack of finance, the ship lay in harbour for almost a year. Then when it was finally afloat it seemed as if all its problems could be put behind them but disaster was lurking in the background. An explosion in the engine room killed several sailors. In 1862 the ship struck an unchartered rock which tore open its hull causing costly damage.

When it was out at sea, the ship's crew began to complain of the deafening hammering sounds that constantly came from the lower decks but for no reason they could work out. The noise was so loud it could be heard above storms and would keep the crew awake at night. Rumours spread that it was made by the ghost of the souls left trapped between the hulls during construction.

The Great Eastern was eventually sold to the government for conversion to a cable-laying ship. Her function was the awesome task of laying a telegraph cable on the seabed from England to America. During this difficult task, men were washed overboard during violent Atlantic storms. Some were killed when the huge cable snapped and some men died trying to pull the severed ends of the broken cable from the bed of the ocean. After several attempts, the cable was successfully laid. The Great Eastern then steamed home to her graveyard, its rusty, haunted hulk sitting moored on the Thames for twelve years until in 1888 the ship was cut up for scrap.

As with her construction, her demolition posed as many problems and progress was slow. When the breakers reached the double-hull, they were greeted by a horrific sight. Trapped between the two iron skins were the skeletons of a man and boy. It is believed these were the riveter and his mate who had not clocked on for work during the ship's construction. Their screams for help would never have been heard above the clash of the hammers and uproar of daily working noises.

Could it be that their appeals for help continued after their death and did the bad luck that seemed to constantly plague the Great Eastern originate from this luckless pair?

Haunted Ships on the Solway

A number of ships are said to haunt the Solway, near Silloth. Whatever the weather, when one particular phantom ship is seen on the Solway, it rolls about as it would in a storm. Ghostly figures are sometimes seen leaning over the sides of the ship which is being tossed about in a very rough sea and at the same time, heart-rendering cries can be heard.

It is thought that the ghost ship is the Rotterdam which sank in the Solway with all hands over a century ago. Since then a ghostly vessel resembling the Rotterdam has been seen in the area it went down. According to an article in the Cumberland News published in 2000, this ghostly vessel shows itself just before a maritime disaster.

This phantom ship has also been linked with the legend of Betsy Jane. This was a slave ship which sank in the Solway near Whitehaven after returning loaded with rare ivory and gold. This had been the reward for shipping load after load of negro slaves. The ghost of the Betsy Jane was only seen in the Solway around December 25th. The ghostly Betsy Jane has also been seen on the approach to Whitehaven Harbour, again around Christmas.

Another ghost ship of a smaller size is said to be a phantom of a barque that was maliciously wrecked in the Solway.

Haunted Places
Ghosts of Huntington Castle

The solid walled fortress that is Huntington Castle stands stark and proud at the end of a long avenue of trees. Built to protect, it may at one time have been impossible for its inhabitants' enemies to get in. But nothing could prevent the building from being impregnated by the essences, wisps and memories that have left their own stamp on its walls, old rooms and dark corridors.

Huntington Castle (also known as Clonegal Castle) is a rambling old mansion that was built in the early 1600s and has been inhabited by the Durdin-Robertson family for more than two centuries. During those centuries it has attracted no fewer than ten phantom presences. Walk this ancient building's mysterious haunted passages in twilight and they will appear to fade away in all directions. As well as having rooms and corridors on eleven different levels, the castle has its own dungeons.

Two of the more predominant ghosts of the castle are believed to be the great grandmothers of one of its owners, L A Durdin-Robertson. One of these ghosts seems to prefer to appear at a particular bush along the 600 year old Yew Walk and the other drifts through the ruins of the ancient chapel at the druids' graveyard.

A ghostly lady has been seen at night strolling by the yews while another shadowy figure often flits in and out of the old ruins. A ghostly soldier from the 17th century has been heard knocking at the door. He was tragically killed by his comrades who didn't recognise him when he returned to the castle because he had disguised himself in his enemy's uniform to spy on them. He was shot through the grille door and now his face sometimes appears together with the sound of knocking, but no-one can be seen standing at the door.

One of the many fascinations of Huntington Castle is its Temple of Isis where followers of Egyptian mythology worship. The sect was started at Huntington by Lord Stathmere and his sister the honourable Olivia Durdin-Robertson. The Temple of Isis occupies the old basement in the castle which is now open to the public.

Ghostly Monks have been seen walking up and down the Yew Walk while the ghostly figure of a girl who is sometimes seen standing by a bush sobbing, is said to be Ailish O'Flaherty, the first wife of Lord Esmonde. So the story goes, she would stand at the bush whenever her husband and son went off to the wars, anxiously watching for their return.

Ghostly Spirits of Skryne Castle

Skryne Castle stands on the slopes of Tara in Ireland at a spot called Skryne or the Hill of the Weeping. It was originally built in 1172 then rebuilt in the nineteenth century close to the place of the Battle of Gowra.

Ghosts that haunt Skryne castle include a woman in white, a tall man with a dog and a nun. Eerie shrieks are often heard in the stillness of a dark night.

The shrieks that can be heard echoing down the corridors of the castle are believed to be those of the ghost of Lillith Palmerston. Her spirit takes many forms including perhaps the woman in white who appears to run through the castle grounds at night clutching her throat.

Lilith Palmerston was in the care of the wealthy landowner who occupied the castle in the 1740s. She spent some time in Dublin then returned to Skryne Castle to live with her guardian. Her beauty was a legend in the district and she attracted the unwelcome attentions of a wealthy squire, Phelim Sellers, who lived on the adjoining estate.

This man tried to woo the young girl but she wasn't interested. He did not like being rejected and decided if the girl would not come to him willingly he would force his attentions upon her. To escape his unwelcome advances, Lilith decided to return to Dublin. News of her intended departure must have reached her admirer for on the night she was planning to leave, Sellers made his way to the castle, forced entry, and found the young girl's bedroom.

The terror-stricken girl fought her uninvited visitor. In fact she was fighting for her life for the squire, angry at her reaction, strangled her in his fury. He was later hanged for the crime in Galway city.

It is thought that the ghost that roams the corridors and castle grounds in the stillness of night is the tormented spirit of Lilith Palmerston who was short-changed, in her lifetime, by this lecherous neighbour.

Wicked Jimmy: the Ghost of Lowther Castle

Only when the conditions are right, Wicked Jimmy, the ghost of Lowther Castle is said to make his appearance. It is always on the anniversary of his burial and only if there's a full moon. This is when, seated high on a carriage, he can be seen riding at a crazy speed through the grounds.

Who is Wicked Jimmy? This ghost is thought to be Sir James who inherited the estate in the late 1700s. He was a greedy man who thrived on power. An arranged marriage brought him more wealth but he wasn't happy with his wife and fell in love with the daughter of one of his tenant farmers. Since he was already married and it wouldn't be suitable anyway for a man of his status to mix socially with someone so beneath him, he took the young girl on as his mistress.

She seemed to be content with this arrangement; at least she had no complaints about the luxurious lifestyle they shared. But one day she fell to her death in a tragic accident. Other rumours suggest she missed her family so much that she died of a broken heart. Whatever the cause of her death, Sir James could never accept losing her this way and the tragic loss of his lover mentally unhinged him. He would not let anyone refer to her as being dead and acted as if she was still alive.

He refused to have her buried as he couldn't bear to be apart from her. According to legend he kept her body in the castle and would dress her himself to sit her at the dining table. In the night he would dress her body in nightwear and lie her on the bed. Finally the smell became so unbearable that he had the corpse moved to a nearby building, placed it in a glass coffin and kept it in a cupboard so he could still visit her regularly.

On his death, locals rejoiced. He could be reunited with his lover. His mistress could be buried at last and they would no longer have to suffer his madness. But perhaps they spoke too soon for his ghost, it is said, continues to haunt Lowther Castle.

Haunted Edinburgh

So far as haunted places go, Edinburgh seems to have more than its fair share of ghosts and hauntings! There can be a spine-chilling creepiness when wandering around Scotland's Capital city's dark alleyways at night. Charlotte Square Gardens, home to the annual Edinburgh Book Festival has several ghosts. A Monk haunts the Square and people often report hearing the sound of a piano playing but no-one knows where the music is coming from.

The ghost of Liberton House was captured on photograph and the picture was published in the Scotsman in 1936. A fire in the house in 1991 seems to have killed sightings of the ghost but its voice can still be heard. There are also regular problems with electrical equipment that cannot be explained.

Edinburgh Castle is considered to be one of the most haunted places in Scotland. In the dungeons of the castle, countless prisoners have died some horrible deaths through many wars. During a research project at the start of the new millennium, 250 visitors who had no previous knowledge of the castle's history, pinpointed areas where they had feelings of a presence and these linked with places that were already know to have paranormal activity.

At Holyrood House, the Queen's official residence in Scotland, the Grey Lady is just one of a number of ghosts that have been seen through the years. She is said to be the spirit of one of Mary Queen of Scot's companions and seems to like to show herself in the Queen's Audience Chamber.

The Ghostly Mary King's close

One of the most spooky places in Edinburgh is Mary King's Close which was a street back in the 17th century and now lies beneath the City Chambers, virtually intact. When the Council was building the Royal Exchange which is now the City Chambers, the houses at the top of Mary Kings close were knocked down but some of the lower sections of the street were left as they were and used as foundations for the new building.

According to the legends, the Close was named after the daughter of the owner of the property Alexander King. In the mid-17th Century Edinburgh became infested with rats from ships in the docks and they spread disease. An attempt was made to contain the plague and subsequently the entrances to Mary King's close were blocked up. Those who had the plague are said to have been left there, to die.

Eventually the Close was reopened and this is when ghosts and other supernatural occurrences were reported. People saw ghostly shadows and headless animals. One woman woke up to find her home filled with phantom-like beings. In recent years the most frequent sighting is of a young girl called Annie. Apparently it was in 1992 when a Japanese psychic who was on a tour of the rooms was suddenly struck by an overwhelming feeling of illness, cold and hunger. When she turned to leave she felt a ghostly hand tug her leg.

The ghost was linked to Annie, a young girl who it is believed was left by her family in Mary King's Close to die. Her plight has touched the hearts of many, and people from all over the world have sent gifts to Annie. These now lie in the corner of a room in Mary King's Close where her ghost is most likely to be spotted. This is so she has toys to play with and need not feel alone.

Some visitors it is said, have reported that photographs they have taken in the underground chambers were washed out or there was no image at all but this is just rumour and since visitors aren't allowed to take photographs while on tours of Mary Kings Close because it is a government owned building, it is hard to say whether this can be true. Tourists who visit this underground 17th century street, can purchase photographs of themselves in the Close, taken by an official photographer.

The Ghost of Cartmel Fell

A ghost of a young girl sitting wistfully on a stone has been seen on Cartmel Fell. Some witnesses report having heard her call a man's name. She is thought to be Kitty Dawson and hers is a very sad tale.

Two farming families on Cartmel Fell were about to be connected by marriage. Kitty Dawson was looking forward to her wedding to her young man, a charcoal burner. But one day, while he was sitting on a stone watching his fire, her lover was struck by lightning.

Kitty was so distraught by her loss and the loss of the future they had planned together that immediately after his funeral she went to his hut and refused to ever leave it again. She sat there, hour after hour, day after day, on the stone where he had sat when he'd met his doom. Her worried family and neighbours brought her food and warm blankets but they could not persuade her to return home.

Then one day during the cold, snowy winter, some men went to her with provisions and found her lying dead, by the stone. Since then, hikers and other people passing the spot have reported seeing a ghostly figure of a young maiden sitting silently on the stone. Some have heard her calling out for her lover.

Phantom Islands

Can Islands appear and disappear at will? According to some Irish legends, the answer is yes! A number of phantom islands in the coastal areas of Western Ireland will show themselves without warning at various times. They are believed to be the homes of fairies and supernatural beings of all kinds. The islands aren't just sighted by one person at a time. Several reports of sightings of these ghostly islands by as many as three hundred people make these mystic appearances more appealing.

Hy-Brasil is the most famous of these islands and long ago, according to legend, this was home to the Fir Bolg and the Formorians. In Celtic forklore, this island takes its name from Breasal, the High King of the Underworld. This island did appear on ancient maps from 1325 and into the 1800s. It was located approximately 200 miles off the west coast of Ireland in the North Atlantic Ocean. Tales about the island included that it was the promised land of Saints or it was a paradise inhabited by an advanced civilisation.

The island was described in some detail by St Brendan who is said to have sailed to America long before Columbus. He actually claimed to have visited the island and was overwhelmed by its beauty and its wealth of inhabitants. Also, according to this Irish saint, Breasail's demise was caused by an excess of sinful living and the negative forces that built up by the islanders caused its destruction.

This island, which seems to have vanished, is said to be hidden in mist but for one day every seven years when it becomes visible. It has been seen from the south-west coast of Ireland and other tales suggest its appearance seems to warn of an impending tragedy such as a shipwreck.

Many of the villagers of Carrigaholt in County Clare witnessed the appearance of a phantom island in 1879. Witnesses described seeing an island rise from out of the sea on a bright sunny day. The island was described in detail by those who saw it. Apparently on its shore's edge was a city of many buildings. Some have pointed out that a city to the people of rural island in the 1800s could have meant anything from a few stone cottages so this probably wasn't as vast as a 21st century city but certainly the description suggests a cluster of buildings.

One afternoon in the summer of 1878 the whole village of Ballycotton in County Cork watched as an island grew before their eyes. At first the island appeared as a distant haze in the sun which could have been mistaken for a mirage but then, as the haze dispersed, the island could be seen quite clearly. In fact some described it as being as clear as their own surrounding landscape. It had a rugged terrain, part was woodland and part was of rocks. One rock rose sharply from the sea than gradually sloped down to a meadow which ran to the sea's edge.

The sighting caused such a stir of excitement that all the boats that could be found in the area, almost one hundred of them, were put out to sea to investigate. This was a time when villagers relied on the sea for their livelihood. Fisherman knew the coast well and it was bound to cause quite a stir that an island had suddenly appeared right over their best fishing ground!

They set off to investigate with a mix of anticipation and curiosity. There was much talk, excitement, shouting and a sense of wonder as the boats approached the mysterious island. But as they got closer, the island became hazy and started to fade away.

The boats never managed to reach the island but all who had set off swore, on their return, that it really had been there. All the villagers who had seen it backed their claims and for the inhabitants of Ballycotton, the Enchanted Isle was indeed, for them, a reality.

Of course, since the sighting, tales have exaggerated the appearance of the island which seems to have grown at each telling. Some describe it as being huge with castles, cities, villages and harbours. The Irish are known for their imaginations and such a tale could lead into some fantastic plots for those who enjoy telling a good story. Even so, the fact remains: this island was documented on old maps and a whole village witnessed the appearance of an island and swore of its existence to the day they died.

In 1882 the people of Ballyheige in Kerry saw an island, just off Tralee Bay. Descriptions of the island were very similar to the one seen by those in Ballycotton and this island, so it is said, appeared to be less than a mile away from the shore. It had fewer trees and wasn't as large as the Ballycotton Enchanted isle, but it was very like it.

While one mysterious island has appeared several times around the mouth of the river Shannon. Are these islands one and the same that keeps appearing in different places, or are they independent of each other? According to Irish legend, it is the same island, the appearance of which is changed by the "Enchanter" so it cannot be recognised and appropriated by claimants.

The island appearing at the mouth of the river Shannon at Ballybunion was not just seen by witnesses but two men are said to have landed on the island too.

David O'Leary and Sean Kelly claim to have landed their fishing boat on this island in 1883. The island had appeared, very much like the others, to a nu mber of people who all set out on boats to try to reach it. The island seemed very close to the shore and the two fishermen decided to head for the left side of the island whereas the others approached the centre or to the right.

The other fishermen claimed later that when they approached the island it got very misty so they couldn't see anything and they also lost sight of O'Leary and Kelly. They all returned but the two other fisherman weren't with them. Two hours later the two men came out of the hazy sunshine and reached the shore, jumping out of their boats excitedly.

They claimed to have reached the edge of the island and were able to scramble to shore onto a mossy outcrop. They described the mysterious island as being beautiful and lush with a rushing stream coming down from a hilly terrain and flowing into a small pool close to where they had landed. They drank the water and it tasted sweeter than anything they'd ever drunk before.

The island had a mountainous terrain, was lush with shrubs and trees. The tale the two men told became a much talked-about legend of the village and O'Leary and Kelly lived on the reflected glory of being the only known people to have succeeded in landing on one of Ireland's Phantom Islands, for many years to come.

Were these sightings a mirage caused by temperature inversions in the atmosphere that distort rays of light or were their appearances as real as those who witnessed them felt them to be? In the rational 21st century, the scientific explanation could be that they were mirages, but the people of Ireland with their long history of folklore, fairies, enchanted beings and the supernatural, are likely to beg to differ.

Orbs, Spears and Globes of Light on Videos and Photographs

Have you ever taken a photograph to have an orb or strange circular blob show when it shouldn't be there? But it isn't on any other photo where lights and conditions were the same? Or you might blame it on your camera lens being dirty but why isn't it on every photo? Some say that these orbs, that aren't visible with the naked eye, are balls of energy that only appear on photographs.

There are explanations for these orbs and these should be ruled out before classing them as anything supernatural. Possible causes include: dust particles floating in the air, insects and moisture, a trick of the light or marks on the camera's lens.

Consider all logical possibilities and then it is possible that an orb might be some form of electrostatic energy. – Some think these are spirit entities.

The above photograph was taken at Lowther Castle during a Halloween event in October 2012 (not on the night of Halloween). A number of photographs, both inside and outside, taken on that night had orbs. There were no insects on this very cold night, the camera lens was clean and in fact the orbs did not show up on all photographs. They appeared in different places of the photographs so this ruled out a dirty camera lens. Some photos showed a single very clear orb and others had orbs floating around all over the place.

Orbs are being noticed more and more in photography. It could be for the fact that most people now use digital cameras but it could also be that more people are taking photographs. This is a phenomenon that cannot be ignored. Could it be in this Age of Technology that spirits have found a new way to communicate with us? What do they signify? Symbolism is strong in the spiritual world. Dreams, the Tarot, I-ching and other forms of divination and self-understanding are rich in symbolism. We pick up intuitively on symbols as they speak to our subconscious.

Most orbs are complete circles representing unity, oneness and coming together as one. Often it is in places where many people are coming together in a celebratory way that many orbs will show. This is like a message to say there are ways the human and spirit world can unite in harmony and love.

Orbs can be seen in the photograph below, again at Lowther Castle during a Halloween Event, when many people had come together in celebration.

Through Orbs, those in the spirit world can send messages of hope, love, peace and healing to those who need it and are receptive to their visits.

Ghost hunters who capture swirls of mist, orbs, spears of light and globules on videos and photographs will have a strong sense that there has been communication between our world and the spirit world. Serious ghost hunters will consider all possible causes before classing a photograph as being authentic. Orbs usually show up as transparent balls of light that hover above the ground.

Many consider orbs as being the soul or spirit of a human or animal that has passed over to the other side. Ghostly shadows, shapes, mists and vortexes have also been captured on camera that weren't visible to the human eye. Of course not all ghost phenomena show up in photographs. Just as ghosts don't only haunt old castles and buildings. An orb could just as easily show up on a photo of the family sharing a Christmas Dinner or holiday. – Maybe it's time to get out your old albums to check out your photos for ghost anomalies?

Ghostly Presences

Photo: L Webb

This ghostly photograph was taking by a psychic who sensed the energy in the room. Other psychics discussing the photograph felt it was a girl between 11 and 20. She was described as petite, meek and as having a protective energy. Some felt in her nightgown, others mentioned a confirmation gown or wedding dress, lace sleeves, up to the neck style. It's as if she is posing for a photo. The photographer feels it may be her cousin's (whose home this was taken in) angel baby who would be around 11 at the time of the photograph.

Angels, Fairies and Supernatural Beings

Our Celtic ancestors accepted the presence of Fairies, Elves and other unworldly creatures as inhabiting forests, caves and streams as a matter of course. These supernatural beings were seen as a natural part of the landscape. Just as it was believed there were secret doorways and entrances to the "Otherworld" and humans could find themselves in the Enchanted Land of Fairies should they enter through them.

In ancient times, woods, mountains and islands were believed to be the home of fairies and other strange beings. At night especially, ghosts would haunt roads, cemeteries and buildings. Ghosts, they believed, were the souls of people in purgatory who would only find rest when they had accounted for all their sins.

Many people believe that fairies are ghosts. Those living in Ireland, Cornwall and on the Isle of Man for instance will know many a tale about these little creatures or 'wee folk' that both fascinate and terrify those who hear them. Some say Fairies actually refer to themselves as being "immortal spirits, ghosts or shadows."

Piskies, they say, favour the high moorland areas of Devon and Cornwall. They are believed to be small, mischievous and childlike. Piskies (also known as pixies elsewhere) enjoy gathering in large numbers to dance the night away. Legends linked with Dartmoor tell how pixies would disguise themselves as a bundle of rags to lure children to join in with their play. These mischievous beings who were known to mislead travellers have also had their helpful moments. They would for instance help humans in distress and needy widows who needed help with their housework!

Dobbies (elves) of Cumbria

In Cumbria in the early 1900s ghostly little people were known as Dobbies (similar to Leprechauns or Elves elsewhere). Dobbies, a kind of household fairy, would only attach themselves to favoured families. An unspoken agreement between residents of these favoured homes and the Dobbies would ensure their assistance in the home, servants would have an easier life and those living in the home would be ensured that all would go well in the household. All of this for just a bowl of milk and an oat cake to be left every night for the Dobbie.

Should, however, the household fail to meet the Dobbie's simple demands, there would be a penalty. Work done that day such as knitting, sewing, tidying or washing would be undone. Cheese-making and butter-making would go wrong, cooking would burn and bad luck would fall upon those living in the house.

One record of a Dobbie of around 1850 is linked with a man living in Martindale called Jack Wilson. He was returning home one moonlit night on his horse and cart and close to Sandwick Rigg he noticed a large gathering of Dobbies playing games. They spied him as he came towards them and quickly climbed up a little ladder into the sky.

During construction of the Carlisle to Lancaster railway it is said that the disturbance angered the Dobbies and they started pulling down the bridge at Shap! Shap is also associated with a ghostly giant. This ghost is linked with Uther Pendragon, father of King Arthur who, so this story goes, was a giant of a man who was cruel and violent. Apparently he would occupy some of his time by trying to divert the river Eden so it would form a moat for his castle.

Travellers going over Shap on cold, wintry nights have reported seeing a ghostly giant mounted on a mighty horse, travelling at some speed in the distance. Some say this is the ghost of Uther Pendragon who because of his cruelty in life, cannot now find any rest.

Ghostly Giants

Many ghost stories of ancient times spoke of ghostly giants of men who were scarily aggressive and fearsome. No-one was safe outdoors at night as this was the time the dead would stir. People would prefer to stay inside by the fire rather than encounter a ghostly horseman galloping through their village or the spirits that flew through the woods and over rocky landscapes.

Throughout Europe there were variations of the ghostly Wild Hunt tale – a phenomenon experienced far and wide – each local legend weaving aspects of its own history and surrounding landscape into the tale. The Wild Hunt is a ghostly army of spirits and beings that ride through the terrain in the darkness of night. They can be linked with past wars, disasters and the history of a town's people.

These tales have been passed down from one generation to another. They tell of cattle raids, invasions, night raids against homes, lights flickering in the distance and in the woods. Voices that spoke a different language as enemies from afar travelled by the light of the moon have also added to legends of the ghostly Wild Hunt.

During the Middle Ages, a man told a tale of a ghostly sighting he had witnessed that still sends shivers down people's spines. He was out one night and heard the sound of an army getting closer. He was then approached by a ghostly giant of a man who told the observer to stay very still and say nothing as he watched the eerie scene.

He saw his dead neighbours and other supernatural beings. He saw women riding side-saddle on saddles that were studded with hot nails, apparently a penance for their previous lifestyle of debauchery. Other groups included land owners and churchmen all being tortured for their various crimes. This is similar to the tales of the ghostly Wild Hunts that haunted many a village throughout Europe.

Ghost Tale or Fairy Tale?

Ghosts of St Michael's Mount, Cornwall

Standing high on a rocky crag, St Michael's Mount which can be seen from miles around, can be accessed along a causeway that links this lofty castle with the mainland. Built in the 12th century, the castle has been in the St Aubyn family since the 1600s.

Cornwall is one of the places in the UK that has been long associated with fairies, pixies, elves and giants and it is said that the Mount itself was constructed by a giant. According to legends, King Arthur once fought a giant on this rocky coast line. And it is a legend linked with St Michael's Mount that is also the source of the well-known fairy tale "Jack and the Beanstalk."

Jack, so the legend goes, is a brave hero who came to St Michael's Mount to rid the place of a ferocious giant called Cormoran. This seventeen feet tall giant terrified people living in the area by his savage and unruly behaviour. Every night he would leave his home at the top of St Michael's Mount to wade across to the mainland where he would plunder cattle and reap havoc around the homes of those living on Cornwall's South West coast.

The brave young man swam over to St Michael's Mount, dug a very deep pit, covered it with sticks and earth and once the trap was set, lured the giant down. Cormoran fell into the trap and Jack killed him. Thus Jack became known as "Jack the Giant Killer" and he was sought out by those being terrorised by giants to rid various places of the massive creatures.

King Arthur, so the legend goes, made Jack a Knight of the Round Table and his task was to rid Wales of all its giants. One particular two-headed giant was determined to make the noble knight suffer for having slaughtered his kinsmen.

But Jack had been rewarded, during his adventures, with a sword that cut through anything, a cap that made him all-knowing, a pair of shoes which enabled him to outrun anyone or anything and a coat that made him invisible. – These were all to his advantage when fighting the gruesome giants.

So thanks to all his magical tools, the vengeful giant Thundel could not see Jack but he could smell the young man. And as Jack approached Thundel, the giant would utter a now well-known warning: "Fe, fi, fo fum, I smell the blood of an Englishman. Be he alive or be he dead, I'll grind his bones to make my bread." Of course, this did not scare off the brave hero and he lured the giant into a booby trapped drawbridge which threw the giant into a deep moat where Jack quickly beheaded him.

Did Jack have a Happy Ever After ending? Was this a Fairy Tale or is the story true? This legend was already six hundred years old before it became popularly known around the country in the 18th century. The story ended after Jack's final adventure when he rescued a fair maiden from a castle on a mountain top where a wicked wizard kept her captive. According to the story, her father was so delighted he granted Jack her hand in marriage. King Arthur presented the newly-weds with a vast estate on their wedding and the couple lived happily ever after.

Ghostly Angels

Angels, like ghosts, are believed to be made up of spirit energy. They have a free choice to do whatever they wish. Angels that are Heavenly in nature have chosen to guard over the lives of those who might need them, thus being known as Guardian Angels. Ghost Angels are highly evolved spiritually because they know the secrets of the Universe. Some people will describe having a spirit guide who will be with them through their life, making them feel protected.

Others believe that Guardian Angels have never been souls of people but are a very separate spirit entity that is allocated to a person to be their passive guide through life. According to this belief everyone can have up to four Guardian Angels with them but they won't interfere with your life. If you feel you need help from your Guardian Angel, you should ask for it. Only then will they intervene and get a message across to you that will be a response to this request or to save you from an impending disaster.

Melinda from Arizona for instance reported of a phase in her life when she had to do a lot of driving every day. One night she was returning home exhausted, trying not to fall asleep when she was suddenly awakened by the loud honking of a car horn. She turned to see the occupants of a car waving to her and then the next moment, the car had gone.

There were no exits and nowhere for the vehicle to have turned off the road. Later she could not reason why the passengers in the car were waving at her and it felt to her as if it had been an angel's car warning her to stay awake. Had they left her with her eyes closed she would have been heading for a nasty accident.

Was it Melinda's Guardian Angel who had helped keep her awake at that crucial time that day or could it have been a ghostly vehicle with the same intention?

Real Ghost Stories (iii) Amazing Paranormal Stories and Investigations

Have you ever heard a bump in the night and felt the hair stand up on the back of your neck, wondering what caused it? Has the door opened or closed on its own when there was no-one else in the room? Did you catch a shadow or movement out of the corner of your eye only to find nothing there or felt the temperature drop significantly for no real reason?

Ghosts and haunted happenings can occur at any time during the night and day and have been reported in many different settings: homes, places of work, ancient buildings, on country roads. There are many types of ghosts and hauntings and some people seem more sensitive to paranormal experiences than others.

Paranormal research is big business now with many organisations offering the chance for people to take part in organised ghost hunts. Some are seriously interested in investigating the paranormal, others it has to be said, have jumped on the bandwagon and are more interested in making money out of a growing fascination with the paranormal. So how can you tell whether a paranormal investigator is for real and what might you expect to experience during a paranormal investigation? This section of my book will give you an idea of what is typically involved in paranormal investigations and what to be wary of.

Also, drawn from literary and internet sources, local records and reports, as well as personal visits and interviews, this part of the book will delve into ghost stories and investigations that have been carried out in some of the most haunted places in the UK.

Covering haunted theatres, castles, underground bunkers and buried streets, this is a great guide for anyone interested in ghost stories or the paranormal adventure wanting to do a little ghost-hunting of their own.

Taking part in Ghost Hunts

It's almost fashionable now for ancient buildings to be haunted. Some will capitalise on this, arranging their own ghost night events and eerie evenings. Many now have their own resident psychic. The sceptic might question whether the psychic feels obliged to provide paying-guests with what they are expecting even if they're unable to pick up a presence on that particular evening. After all, who would be able to tell the difference?

If you're looking to take part in a ghost hunt in your area, many now charge you for the privilege. It is true that paranormal investigators have to earn a crust just like everyone else so warnings about not going with anyone who charges for a ghost hunt are somewhat extreme. However do some research into the background of the organisation as there will be people out there who will do all in their power to provide the experience you want and this makes them no better than frauds.

Gadgets used within these investigations can give a degree of scientific proof as long as common-sense explanations are also considered. A sudden drop in temperature for instance could be put down to a sudden draught coming in through a window. Remember too that the equipment is only as scientific as the person using it.

An Ouija board is not scientific. It might be used in conjunction with technical equipment to seek spiritual or telepathic messages but these can leave more questions than answers. What if someone was deliberately moving the planchette or pointer? Could it have been influenced by your subconscious mind?

If the Ouija board does happen to pick up an otherworldly presence, could a malevolent spirit be masquerading as a good one and stick around to cause emotional damage to those taking part in this séance? Remember there is a difference between investigating paranormal activity and inviting spirits to talk to you. This also brings in the use of psychic mediums during paranormal investigations.

It is now standard practice to take a medium along on a ghost hunt. And it will be rare that a medium does not pick up on some form of presence. This adds to the atmosphere and entertainment of the ghost hunt but it is not absolute proof of a haunting. Genuine psychics will direct other investigators in the right directions but the main thrust of any paranormal investigation should be to prove findings and gain credibility through scientific evidence.

It can be fascinating to hear a psychic describe what they pick up during a ghost hunt and it may be possible to confirm names later but a paranormal investigation relying primarily on a medium to do all the work is not entirely scientific.

How is Paranormal Activity Investigated?

Serious paranormal investigations are similar to police and legal investigations. Once the ghost sighting, haunting or supernatural activity has been reported, investigators might meet up with witnesses, take statements and visit the venue to gather evidence.

Different organisations have their own methods of investigation. Some will involve a select team of experienced ghost-hunters, some invite people to join them in their investigations. Techniques vary depending on individual preferences, location and who else is involved.

Investigations can include: lone vigils, group observations, séances and mediums. Scientific equipment used in ghost hunting and paranormal investigations might include: cameras and videos, TVs, audio recording devices or digital sound recorders, EMF meters, thermometers, computer software and electronic sensors. Psychic equipment may include dowsing rods, scrying mirrors and pendulums that measure magnetic changes in the air and earth.

After receiving a report of a haunting or a request to look into ghostly sightings, investigators are likely to interview witnesses and ask for any evidence they may have to support their claim. They may for instance have photographs, videos or recordings that can help explain their paranormal experience.

Next the investigators will decide whether this is a situation worth investigating and how they might go about it. They will need to decide how many will take part in the investigation, arrange a date and time of arrival that gives them plenty time to set up equipment before the actual vigil takes place. During the investigation, evidence will be gathered. Afterwards, photographs, videos, results of the audio and sensor readings and personal observations will all be analysed and conclusions formed from these.

There are different levels of Paranormal Research groups. Some organisations involve serious academic/scientific research, publish journals, have their own websites and employ investigators with scientific/technical backgrounds. Other groups are made up of people interested in helping to research the paranormal who take photographs, record their experiences and form conclusions based on their personal experiences.

The aim of a ghost hunt or paranormal investigation is to verify or debunk a report of past supernatural activity having taken place at a particular venue. The goal is to find an explanation for what occurred, whether this is a paranormal one or not. It has to be accepted too that investigators may come away admitting that some strange things may have occurred but no cause for this has yet been found.

The most obvious explanations should be examined first. If for instance a door keeps closing, is there an open window nearby causing a draught? If walls or floorboards are creaking, could this be water pipes cooling? If it is an open window that may be causing doors to close or objects to move, once the window is closed the door should be observed. If it still closes on its own is there another explanation?

Ghost hunting is serious business. Anyone taking part should not be going along to play practical jokes on others. If you start taking part in regular investigations, take along a notebook and afterwards record your thoughts/experiences, photographs and other evidence methodically.

It is also important to gain permission before entering private property.

Points to consider on a ghost hunt:

If you're on a ghost hunt you might bear in mind the following practical tips:

- It's not a good idea to go ghost-hunting alone especially in secluded places.
- Make sure you charge batteries in all electronic equipment to be used, beforehand.
- Is your camera lens clean? Marks on the lens can be mistaken for orbs.
- Photographs taken in the rain or fog or when it is snowing can cause strange marks on the image that have nothing to do with ghosts.
- Tell the ghosts why you are there. Invite them to have their photo taken.
- It might be useful to have your mobile phone in your pocket in case you need it.

- Visit the location in daylight hours if possible before the actual investigation.
- Never trespass on private land or property.
- Do not allow anyone to smoke during an investigation,
- Avoid using flash when taking photographs of shiny surfaces, windows etc.
- Useful equipment for a ghost hunt includes: digital camera, audio recording device, notebook and pen, mobile phone, thermometer, a watch to keep tabs on time, First Aid Kit, Electric Magnetic Field detector, torch and extra batteries, warm clothing.

Amazing Paranormal Investigations

Haunted Cinemas and Theatres in the UK

Strange lights, shadowy figures, shouts and screams from an empty building, whispered warnings, weird noises and intense feelings … there's always a guarantee of a dramatic production when visiting cinemas and theatres! But not all the drama is produced for entertainment. Many cinemas and theatres in the UK seem to be the location of a surprising amount of supernatural activity. The type which has attracted the attention of a number of eager ghost hunters.

Ghostly sightings at the Sunderland Royalty theatre, for instance, have been known to seriously creep people out. Here the atmosphere can be both chilling and thrilling when the show goes on even after the curtains close.

The Sunderland Royalty theatre is home of the Sunderland Drama Group. This Victorian building has a ground floor and first floor, a foyer, bar, theatre and rehearsal room. The Drama Group has used the building for fifty years. Prior to this it belonged to the Union Congregational Church. It was also used as a hospital for soldiers during the Second World War.

Footsteps have regularly been heard walking across the empty stage. People have reported seeing ghostly figures at the back of the auditorium. Piano music has been heard playing while lights seem to switch on and off by themselves. Members of the Drama Group have complained about items going missing, only to be found later in another part of the theatre.

A number of paranormal investigations have been carried out at the theatre and the UK Paranormal Study Organisation found a ghost of a man hangs around a specific area in the building a good deal of the time. Shadowy figures have been seen and it is thought that one of the ghosts is someone who died while the theatre was being built. Ghostly guests, it is said, adds to the theatrical esteem of the theatre and they aren't felt to be malevolent.

Still in Sunderland and Molly Mozelle, resident ghost of the Empire Theatre in Sunderland is reported to be seen in the property, usually at postal collection times. She was stage manager of a touring musical and her story is that she was never seen or heard of after going out one afternoon in January 1949 to post a birthday card. She was 33 years old at the time and the card was never received by the intended recipient.

Molly's real name was Mary Burslem, a bubbly girl with a strong personality. But underneath her smiles lay some sadness. According to old newspaper reports, her love life had not been a bed of roses when in 1948, she split up from her comedian partner Bunny Doyle after a 16 year affair. She did find someone new, a businessman, Walter Hatterseley, but unfortunately, this romance ended in tears. Some say she received a letter from Walter on the day she disappeared but this could not be found and the contents – whatever may or may not have been said – can only be left to the imagination.

There was a massive police search extending across the UK for Molly but she was never found and the police file remains open. In the meantime, the ghost that is apparently Molly continues to hang around the theatre. A cleaner employed by the theatre heard Molly's ghost not long after she started working there. While cleaning the seats in the gallery the employee heard scratching noises and moaning. Other members of staff told her it was the ghost of Molly Moselle. The tale she was told was that Molly had been engaged to the leading man of the show "The Dancing Years," but they fell out and he started an affair with the leading lady of the same show. Apparently, one Saturday after the show, Molly went out to post a letter and was never seen again. The theatre was thoroughly searched by the police and because her handbag and belongings were still in her digs it seemed she wasn't planning to run away. Very mysterious!

Another ghost reputed to haunt the Empire Theatre is that of a female violinist who died on the site. She has been seen drifting along the dress circle before vanishing.

This is the theatre where Carry-on legend Sid James suffered a heart attack during a performance in 1976 and died on the way to hospital. Rumours spread that the dressing room he used on the night of his death was haunted by him; it is also said that after the comedian Les Dawson performed there, he refused to play at the Empire Theatre ever again. Barbara Windsor it is rumoured, also refuses to work there.

The location of the Tyneside Cinema in Newcastle, Tyne and Wear, England was once a monastery dating back to 1267. Rumours tell of the monastery having burnt to the ground with Monks still in the building. A mansion house was also built in the same location in the 1580s. This was later used as a jail in which King Charles I was imprisoned for ten months before his execution. For many years, before the invention of television, the building was used as a News Theatre, a popular means of broadcasting news from around the world to the local community.

With ghostly figures having been seen in the office and stage areas and reports of the sound of Monks chanting in the lower levels of the building not to mention lights turning themselves off and on, this venue has proved a popular location for local paranormal investigation groups to hold ghost hunts. One investigation took place at Halloween in 2003.

During this investigation, an elaborate collection of high-tech equipment was used including motion detectors and sound monitors. A psychic was also present and despite never having been before, he gave information which was recorded and later verified by a historian. A pendulum responded in a corridor to what was believed to be a ghost of a tortured soul and despite no ghostly presence being witnessed, orbs (translucent or solid circles believed to be spirit energy) were captured on photographs.

The Theatre Royal in Newcastle, Tyne and Wear has long had a reputation of being haunted. Originally built in 1837, the interior was gutted by a ferocious fire. This occurred just after a performance of Shakespeare's Macbeth (a play with a reputation for causing misfortune!) Between March and September 2011 the theatre was closed for refurbishment and underwent a £4.75 million restoration.

The theatre's most famous ghost is that of a woman believed to be from the 19th century who it is said fell from the upper circle while reaching out to an actor she was in love with who was rehearsing on the stage.

A Paranormal Investigative team spent the night at the Theatre Royal. They took their time setting up the investigation and had a guide show them around the place beforehand. The investigation took place in the seated area of the theatre in dim light. The group split into teams, each team having a medium. Temperature fluctuated, knocks were heard and one of the mediums reported feeling someone who may have had a heart attack but generally it was agreed that there was little activity on that night.

A more successful investigation was carried out by the Paranormal Activity Research Team of Lancashire at the Royal Court Theatre in Bacup. This investigative team experienced a lot of paranormal activity including the sound of shuffling feet as if people were preparing for a performance and sightings of ghostly figures moving about. A ghostly figure has been captured, in colour on a photograph taken in the theatre. The ghost is almost see-through and out of proportion with other people on the photo.

Another theatre in the North East of England where evidence has been gathered of paranormal activity is the Town Hall Theatre in Hartlepool. This gothic-style building was built in 1896 and although primarily a theatre, it has been used by a nearby college. The rooms that were used as classrooms are now being used as dressing rooms.

While in these rooms, people have reported feeling strange, sensing an eerie presence and having weird sensations that make them uneasy. A manager of the theatre who can usually walk happily through any building in pitch darkness without any problems, claims to have to sometimes turn the lights on while locking up the Theatre. For while in the darkness he has felt a sense of foreboding and of not being alone. Noises that would seem to point to human activity have been reported from areas of the theatre where no-one happened to be. A group investigating the building has recorded ghostly voices which they think may be linked with a technician who centred his life on his job at the Theatre.

Moving into Scotland and the conclusion arrived at by the Mostly Ghostly Haunted Theatre Tour Team, after carrying out a number of paranormal investigations at the Theatre Royal in Dumfries, was that they'd experienced unusual happenings for which they could not at the time explain. Their aim is to gather evidence of paranormal activity, and witness reports speak of footsteps being heard on the balcony, flickering lights have been observed and a ghostly women in a flower patterned dress was seen falling down a set of stairs. People have noticed a sudden drop in temperature, one visitor felt their hand being held while another felt their hand being squeezed.

During one experiment while on the stage, they asked that a ghost might respond with a whistle and a clear whistle was heard by sixteen people.

Paranormal Investigations at Mary King's Close, Edinburgh

Mary King's Close is a fascinating underground 17th century street lying beneath the Royal Exchange in Edinburgh (see Part III of this book). It remains largely intact, being used as foundations for the existing building. When the plague struck the community living in this area, the Council bricked off the street to leave the inhabitants who had the plague to die inside.

Open to visitors, it is best to book well-ahead for anyone wanting to visit as it is an enormously popular tourist attraction. Guides, dressed in costume and taking on roles of characters who lived in the street at the time, lead visitors down the steps to these ancient houses that open out onto a steep narrow lane exactly as it would have been in the 1600s. Photography isn't allowed because this is a government building.

It is believed the Close which is also known as the Street of Sorrows, was named after a daughter of the owner of the property, Alexander King. Although this is not a certainty, a woman called Mary King did live in the Close in the mid-17th century.

Among the ghostly experiences reported are headless animals and disembodied people, eerie cries and shadowy figures along the alleyway. The most famous ghost of the Close is that of a young girl aged around five who has been affectionately named as Annie.

In 2010 the Scottish Paranormal Charity held an investigation into what is believed to be paranormal activity in Mary Kings Close. Equipment used by the team included night vision camcorders, temperature probes, laptops, a DVR system, cameras, digital recorders and a sound mixer/microphone. Equipment was set up in a base room before the group went further into the Close to carry out the investigation. Firstly they visited a room at the top of the close in one of the more wealthy homes compared with those living in the lower more cluttered areas of the Close. The temperature did drop after a while and footsteps were heard outside the room although there was no-one there.

In the room where a merchant, Alexander Cant was said to have been murdered by his wife and mother-in-law, one of the group reported feeling nauseous and someone heard a knocking sound that could not be explained. Not everyone felt uneasy in this part of Mary Kings Close despite its murderous connections.

In the cattle shed, and the plague room next door, many reported a pungent smell. (This smell is not always there and I wasn't aware of it when visiting Mary Kings Close in 2012).

The plague room is closed to visitors although they can look inside where there is a cloaked figure of a doctor standing over the model of a young boy who is dying of the plague. Another model representing his mother is sitting on a hard bed holding a dying child in her arms. During the investigation, the investigative team were allowed in this room. Here, the needle of the EMF meter went off the scale and it was believed this was caused by overhead pipes and cables. Many found the smell horrible and yet as mentioned this room can be visited at times when there is no smell at all.

In the plague room, three of the group thought they heard a child's voice. One heard the sound of footsteps coming from somewhere else in the Close.

The most famous ghost of Mary Kings Close is Annie who has even been featured on Billy Connolly's World Tour of Scotland. Apparently a Japanese medium picked up on Annie's lonely ghost while visiting the Close and now people from all over the world send gifts of toys for Annie, all of which are kept in her room. According to one of the guides who shows visitors around, there was a girl called Annie who was the daughter of a merchant who lived in that house. However historic evidence does not support this. No proof has been found of a girl living in there called Annie who'd been left to die as many say Annie had been.

The investigative team in Annie's room on this occasion recorded some drop in temperature. One person saw a strange light hovering over a teddy bear which was on the pile of toys in the corner of the room. But no-one else saw this and it was not recorded on the camcorder which was being used that evening.

There are people who claim to have captured a ghostly voice while recording in Annie's room but apart from the eerie feelings and apparent ghostly sightings, some ghost investigators believe that Annie's story is more hype than actual paranormal activity.

A Mr Chesney was the last person to have left Mary Kings Close. He lived in what looks like a large house with its door leading onto the alleyway. For health and safety reasons tourists aren't allowed within and can only glimpse the wide passageway that leads to the downstairs room while the guide stands at his door, telling his tale. Mr Chesney stubbornly remained in the Close and when eventually was forced to go, he took the door knocker from his door.

The investigative team were allowed inside. Here a knocking noise was captured on camcorder rather like something being dropped down the stairs and this could not be accounted for. Other noises were picked up which as yet have had no explanation. For anyone visiting Edinburgh who is interested in ghosts or history, Mary King's Close is well worth a visit.

Is Scotland's Secret Bunker Haunted?

Another underground location that is said to be haunted is Scotland's Secret Bunker. Here, underneath an innocent looking bungalow there lies a huge underground command bunker which was designed to accommodate three hundred people and withstand nuclear attack. – Another fascinating place to visit.

Kept secret for many years, the Bunker is now open to the public. Entrance is through the bungalow which also acts as a guard house. There are two levels and one is encased in 15 feet of reinforced concrete, one hundred feet below ground.

Within its labyrinth of tunnels, there are six dormitories, communications rooms, an emergency broadcasting studio, information room, Commissioner's room, conference room, cinemas, dining rooms, a small chapel and a board room where important decisions would have been made.

As well as military personnel there would have been people manning the fully equipped BBC sound studio for emergency broadcasts.

Visitors have reported hearing unexplained footsteps, feeling a sudden drop in temperature and seeing flickering lights and shadows. Ghostly sightings involve figures in uniform spotted in various areas. Footsteps and voices have been recorded during paranormal investigations and strange lights captured on photographs. Visitors have reported noticing orbs on their photographs and one person witnessed a ghostly figure on one of the stairwells.

(A Stairwell within the Bunker. Note orb on the bottom right of photograph)

The first paranormal investigation of the secret bunker was carried out in 2005. While in the stairwell, a medium with the group could sense a presence and mentioned the name of an RAF serviceman. The needles on the EMF meters were going crazy but they weren't far from the BT services room where there is a high voltage distribution unit mounted on the wall. So this was the probable cause of the high readings.

The presence of two Spaniels was sensed by the medium in a display room, strange smells were noticed by the switchboard and a small man was sensed in the Telex room. Most strange were the sensations the medium got from the Chapel which seemed almost mischievous. He felt the chapel was most likely used for fun antics by the men than for worship. The medium sensed a fight between two men over a woman in the small store at the rear of the coffee shop and it was confirmed that this room had been originally a part of the accommodation. Ghostly presences were also sensed by the medium in one of the cinemas and one of the dormitories.

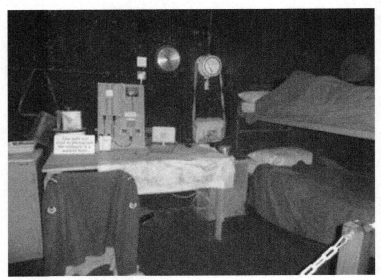

(Dormitory in the bunker: note orb in top right corner)

During the investigation, one of the group saw lights under the staircase where a previous visitor had seen the man on the stairs. Video footage and photographs showed nothing unusual. Faint noises were heard by the group when the medium asked if one of the spirits he could sense to be there might confirm its presence by making a noise. There was a noted drop in temperature while this was happening.

During the vigil in the Chapel, members of the group felt lower back pain when any presence was asked to contact the team by making a noise or touching someone. No movement was recorded on the trigger object yet a church hymnal was found lying open on top of the organ keyboard whereas this had been originally closed. No-one admitted to having opened it.

Chapel: Is this a place of Ghostly Mischief?

Although the medium contacted a number of entities, little solid evidence was gathered during this vigil. Some of the group had seen and felt sensations that could not be explained but scientifically, there was little to suggest proof of any supernatural activity.

In 2008 another investigation took place. During this investigation mediums picked up on various spirit entities and their names in different areas of the bunker. Twice the face-recognition feature of one of the investigator's cameras was switched on while he was taking photographs but he had not done this. When he noticed this, it then switched itself off!

The sound of voices and muffled conversation was heard in the corridors although no-one was there. A door was seen to open slightly and a grey figure was seen.

(Corridor: note orb on bottom right of photograph)

In the royal observation corps room a mannequin was found to have fallen over since their first visit. Shuffling and rattling sounds were heard. During this investigation members of the group saw shadows and ghostly figures, door handles moving, heard voices and an alarm sounding. Investigating this further, a door in the corridor was seen to close. No one was there. A number of people experienced and witnessed a variety of paranormal activity that night which on careful examination could not be explained.

(Dormitory in the Bunker)

Photographs of the Bunker were taken in 2012 during an afternoon visit. Orbs on some of the photographs were noticed later.

Paranormal Investigations: The Schooner Hotel, Alnmouth

The Schooner Hotel in Alnmouth with its maze of corridors that can leave a visitor feeling totally disorientated is reputed to be one of the UK's most haunted hotels. Investigations by the Poltergeist Society have twice confirmed this and so famous is this place for its hauntings that it has been investigated by a number of top paranormal investigators.

Being officially listed as having over sixty spirits and with over 3,000 reported sightings, it seems like a high chance that anyone joining in the ghost-hunts arranged at this hotel is likely to experience some kind of paranormal activity.

Originally built as a Coaching Inn, the hotel dates back to the 17th century. It has been at the centre of the small seaport of Alnmouth for over 300 years. The harbour was once thriving with ships coming from all over the world bringing cargoes of grain and coal. Alnmouth also had a reputation for its less reputable trade: smuggling.

There is no detailed documented history of the hotel but its past has been linked with murders and suicides. If walls could talk, those within this building would have a few gruesome tales to tell! Throughout its history people have reported seeing ghosts, hearing strange noises and sensing otherworldly presences in its rooms.

Apparently a number of famous people have stayed there through the centuries including Charles Dickens, Douglas Bader and King George III. The hotel even has its own resident medium: Ray Bokor. He organises regular ghost hunts and paranormal investigations. During one of many investigations with a small group of people, one woman looked into a mirror to see her face change into a man's while another guest saw her face change to a young girl.

Just before Halloween in 2011 a family took part in one of Ray Bokor's ghost hunts. They were shown around the hotel with Ray picking up names and events linked with the visitors. In room 17 the family were encouraged to use an ouija board while the medium captured the experience on video. The glass did move and a name was given. Other spirits who came through were late relatives of the family who gave information no-one else knew. Further into the night the family split up and two of them sat in a room in the dark with their video camera. They did not think there was anything in the room and yet on playing back the footage on returning home, a white shadow walks into the room to the window and back out again with its arm swinging back and forth.

In room 28, it is said that a family was murdered. Screams have been heard from this room. In room 17 a young boy's ghost apparently rides his trike, banging against the door and all along the corridor are scratches on the doors that cannot be explained. Rooms 28, 29 and 30 are the most noted for the strange noises and whispers coming from within. Dark shadows have been seen.

(Orb outside room 19, Schooner Hotel)

A guest in room 5 heard continual unexplained noises that went on until the early hours of the morning. In 2011 a group of friends stayed in room 28. Items moved, messages appeared on the mirror and creaks sounding like footsteps came from the corridor although no-one was there. A blood-curdling scream was heard around 4 am and yet no-one else in the hotel heard it.

A paranormal investigator attended the Schooner hotel with a group of researchers. He spent some time in the cellar of the Schooner Hotel on his own and recorded some supernatural activity there. At one time the group met in a corridor where they heard a door slam in another part of the hotel. A tall man was seen walking into one of the rooms by one of the group; no-one questioned this at the time until they found out later that everyone who was in the building were in the corridor.

Another paranormal investigator Darren Ritson, described his experience at the Schooner hotel in his book "In Search of Ghosts." He mentioned feeling an 'overwhelming presence' pursuing him near the back kitchen, seeing doors open and close by themselves and hearing disembodied footsteps and other inexplicable noises.

One of the Schooner's ghosts is a woman who is believed to have committed suicide after receiving news that her husband had died while working overseas. According to legend, the woman stabbed herself in the abdomen with a long-bladed knife. She died instantly, as did her unborn child. The blood curdling screams that are heard at night in the hotel are believed to be hers.

Some of the many ghosts that are said to haunt the Schooner Hotel include a man who murdered his family in one of its rooms, a parson who died after being struck on the head by an exploding beer tap and a small girl.

The TV series "Most Haunted" investigated the Schooner Hotel and their findings can be seen in its Series 3 (2003) footage.

Supernatural Activity at Jedburgh Castle Jail

It isn't surprising that some paranormal activity has been recorded at Jedburgh Castle Jail, a place of cruelty, misery and executions. Built on the site of the original Jethart Castle which was destroyed in the early 1400s to prevent it from falling into the hands of the English, the Jail was built in 1823 to house male and female criminals. These included youngsters who were believed to have committed crimes. Children too would spend time in the prison alongside their mothers.

Ghosts have not only been seen but heard here when visitors have reported a feeling of being followed while walking around the building. Or as if someone was standing next to them even though no-one was there. Ghostly footsteps walking around the corridors have been heard as well as the sound of doors banging and someone whistling. A ghost piper has been seen on the battlements.

It hasn't just been in modern but in ancient times that ghosts have been seen in this area. In 1285 King Alexander III saw a ghostly figure in a black hooded cloak, wearing a mask in the castle. This figure was seen again just before the battle of Flodden Field and was believed to be an omen of death and disaster.

Five executions were held in this prison that comprised three separate blocks. One was for females (including their children) and debtors, another for correction and the last for prisoners who had committed more serious crimes. The last person executed was Thomas Wilson for the murder of a shepherd at St Boswell's Fair. Later it was discovered he was innocent of this crime.

During overnight vigils, a variety of paranormal activity has been recorded including flickering lights and orbs captured on photographs, sounds of creaking doors and poltergeist activity. One ghost hunter who spent some time in a cell on his own reported to having had, what felt like pebbles thrown at him.

Members from the Glamorgan Paranormal Society carried out an investigation in the Castle Jail in 2004 and according to their reports "Encountered endless scares." The investigator who'd spent time alone in a cell in the dark and had pebbles thrown at him actually picked this up on recordings. Unexplainable flashing lights were also seen in the same cell.

In another cell, a flashlight switched off by itself when the group entered and then back on again as they left. No other equipment would work in that cell.

In 2009 a team of paranormal investigators from the West Midlands visited Jedburgh Castle Jail. For them, the most eerie experiences were felt in the Children's part of the prison where a medium picked up on some of the many children who had died of sickness and illness in this section of the building. During another investigation in the previous year, one woman felt as if she was being strangled while another felt physically sick when visiting the Women's Wing. Someone called James was contacted during a séance who it was discovered had spent a decade in the jail. A floating spirit was captured on video and dowsing rods would spin madly in one cell but remained quiet in other rooms. This had a sceptic investigator intrigued. Never having experienced this before he kept returning to the cell where the rods would spin.

During another investigation in 2008 by twelve members of the Ghost Club, spirit lights were witnessed by most members of the team. These were described as being like fairy lights twinkling on a Christmas tree, appearing and disappearing. The cell where this was experienced was thoroughly checked and no explanation for the lights could be found. Investigators also witnessed shadows very much like experiences that had already been reported by prison staff.

One group all clearly head the sound of doors banging below them, similar to cell doors being slammed shut. There was a feeling among some, that they were being watched and as if unseen presences were around them. Fleeting, moving shadows were seen at the end of one corridor but on going to investigate, noises would transfer themselves to the other end of the corridor as if some unseen ghostly presence was playing games with them.

In one cell could be heard the sounds of snoring while one person felt someone touch her back. A medium got through to the prisoners who complained about the harsh conditions and overcrowding. Prisoners were cold and hungry all the time.

The Castle Jail is now open to the public as well as being a licensed wedding and civil ceremony venue. It is a popular place for spine-tingling overnight ghost hunts.

Paranormal Investigations: Edlingham Castle, Northumberland

A team of ghost-hunters did not have very high expectations when conducting a paranormal investigation at Edlingham Castle, Northumberland. People visiting the ruins had reported feeling unseen hands tugging at their coats and a medium felt this was the spirit of a young girl with a playful personality who just wanted to get people's attention. There had also been reports of seeing strange lights flitting in and out of the ruins and weird sounds coming from that area.

Built in the 12th century as a House the building was fortified during the unsettled times of the Border Reivers. Over the years the property was improved and defences included a moat, a gatehouse and a tower. The house became known as a castle from around the early 1400s and the castle was abandoned during the English Civil War. Two of its last inhabitants were witnesses to the witch trial of Margaret Stothart, known as the Witch of Edingham. The alleged witch lived in the village in the 1680s. During her trial, witness John Mill of Edlingham Castle testified that while he was lying in bed he heard a strong blast of wind go past his window before something "fell with great weight on my heart and gave a great cry like a cat."

A light appeared at the foot of his bed and within this light he saw Margaret Stothard or her vision. He also described how when he was riding through the village in the night and passing the house where she lived, there was a flash of fire that went to Margaret Stothard's door and his horse refused to move until he cried upon the Lord.

On the night of the paranormal investigation, almost immediately on their arrival, the three investigators could hear strange noises coming from a nearby field. Nothing could be seen in torch light but the noise, which sounded like heavy breathing, continued. – There were no animals in the vicinity that might account for the sound.

Heading for the ruins, a photograph was taken in the graveyard of the church and it was noticed that a huge bright white expanse rather like steam rising was on the photograph.

Walking towards the ruins the investigators disturbed sheep in the fields so there was quite a lot of noise as the animals here rose from their sleep and headed for other spots to settle. As they reached what would have been the main entrance of the castle, one of the investigators saw a dark figure sitting on the wall but on looking again it had gone. He called to the figure and asked for it to show itself again but nothing happened. All investigators sensed an atmosphere and felt as if they were being watched.

On carefully making their way to the tower they heard what sounded like a large stone being thrown down from the top, bouncing off the walls. The air was oppressive and overwhelmingly eerie. The investigators stood still, lights from their torches moving around the area. Dark shadowy figures were seen by all investigators and the whole atmosphere spooked them so much that one experienced investigator wanted to leave immediately. The others did not take a lot of persuading.

To say they were nervous and spooked by the experience is putting it mildly. But could the noises of stones falling and ghostly sightings have been their imagination playing tricks on them? It was acknowledged that this was a possibility. However not just one but two investigators had seen moving black shadows and one witnessed a strange light. The atmosphere they described as being 'oppressive' and they all had a strong sense of being watched. As they got further away from the ruins, this oppressive atmosphere lifted. Is Edlingham Castle, Northumberland really haunted? ... the conclusion can only be left to further investigations.

And although there are no explanations for hauntings at the castle, could it be the ghost of Margaret Stothard, perhaps still vexed with those who lived at the castle and village of Edingham who accused her of being a witch?

Haunted Muncaster Castle

As well as being one of the best preserved Victorian homes in its area, Muncaster Castle is also one of the most haunted castles in the UK. Visitors shown around some of its magnificent rooms including the great hall, dining room, billiard room, the King's room, library, drawing room and tapestry room will also hear tales of the castle's resident ghost.

A number of paranormal investigations have been carried out at Muncaster in Cumbria. But so far there has been no explanation about the cause of the spooky events that often take place here.

Muncaster Castle's resident ghost is Tom Fool and although he is rarely seen, guides at the Castle will tell of how his spirit is known to play tricks on visitors and staff. He seems to prefer the Tapestry Room and visitors sleeping here have complained of being disturbed in the night by the door handle turning and the door opening but no-one being there.

Tom Fool lived in the late 1500s and was known to have a mischievous nature. His real name was Thomas Skelton and he was employed as the 'fool' or jester of the castle. According to legend, one of Tom's favourite pastimes was to sit under a chestnut tree outside the castle. When travellers passed him and asked for directions to London, he would engage them in conversation to decide whether or not he liked them. If he didn't he'd point them in the direction of the quicksand and marshlands rather than to the road they should be on. It has been said that it was Thomas Skelton's tricks such as this that the phrase 'tom foolery' originated. Also, Tom Fool of Muncaster is said to be the model of the Fool in Shakespeare's "King Lear".

One story tells of how a local carpenter fell in love with the owner of the castle, Sir Pennington's daughter. By orders of Sir Pennington, Tom had to chop off the carpenter's head! To keep his master happy Thomas carried out this brutal murder.

Mischievous also in death, most sinister happenings and paranormal activity at the castle is blamed on Tom Fool.

A child has been heard crying by the window of the Tapestry Room and occasionally a lady can be heard singing as if she is comforting a sick child.

Other ghosts of Muncaster Castle are the White Lady who roams the gardens who also known as the 'Muncaster Boggle'. She is said to be the ghost of Mary Bragg a young girl who was murdered on the road near the Main Gate in the 1800s.

Mary, who lived and worked in Ravensglass was in love with the footman at Muncaster Castle. She was not the only one who had eyes on the footman. One of the housemaids at the castle also fancied the fellow. It is believed that the maid arranged for two men to call at Mary's one night and tell her that her lover was seriously ill. They volunteered to escort her to his bedside but instead of taking her to the castle they led Mary down a lonely road and killed her.

Her body was found weeks later in the River Esk. Her ghost, it is said, is often seen wandering the grounds of the castle while other tales speak of how the tree by which she was murdered began to bleed as it was cut down.

Investigators from Parascience Media Investigations were invited by the BBC's Inside Out program to spend a night in Muncaster Castle. Equipment was set up in all areas where paranormal activity had been reported. During this visit there was an archaeological dig also going on within the castle grounds.

After an evening discussing the castle, paranormal events and ghostly happenings in general, the team began to retire. Within minutes of Ian Aspin, the presenter of the program, retiring to the Tapestry Room he was seen on monitors to be sprinting back down the corridor at some speed. He reported having felt uncomfortable the moment he went into the room and this feeling had progressed very quickly to terror. No paranormal activity was found on the equipment and the rest of the team kindly volunteered to spend the rest of the night in the Tapestry Room with him.

Many visitors have spent the night in the Tapestry Room and Muncaster Castle continues to allow people to stay there. Some have heard the sound of a baby crying or someone softly singing. Dark figures have been seen leaning over some visitors while others have felt a heavy weight falling on top of them while they were lying in the antique four-poster bed.

It isn't surprising to hear that it was found that at one time the Tapestry Room was a children's nursery.

Also, what was discovered during the archaeological dig being carried out at that time (and which is on-going), helps confirm folk tales about the castle having been developed from the medieval core of a Pele Tower which was possibly built on the foundations of a Roman Watch Tower.

Could the dig have awakened an unearthly presence in addition to unearthing traces of a Roman presence in the area? While archaeologist Clifford Jones he was staying in the castle, he heard someone chopping wood one night. There was only himself and one other person staying in the castle. He made his way down to the courtyard towards the noise but when he got there he could see nothing. He called out "Please stop the noise," and it did stop.

Going back upstairs the first room he went into was the toilet and the moment he entered, the light bulb blew. He went to switch on the light in the corridor but that light bulb went 'pop' too. The same thing happened when he went to the lounge.

Clifford was so disturbed by this experience that after leaving the castle it took him three days to build up the courage to return.

Haunted Kielder Castle, Northumberland

Within the beautiful forestry area of Kielder, close to the beautifully tranquil Kielder Dam, stands Kielder Castle. Built in 1775 as a hunting lodge for the 1st Duke of Northumberland it is now owned by the Forestry Commission and for many years during the period, when it was customary for large companies to provide social meeting places for their workers, it was used as a Working Men's Club for the foresters.

Like so many ancient English Castles, Kielder Castle in Northumberland has its resident ghosts and is a popular location for organised ghost hunts.

Despite the beauty and serenity of modern-day Kielder, the place itself has a gory history being on the border of England and Scotland. And like many other areas on the border, its inhabitants suffered through raids, pillages and skirmishes with the Border Reivers. It wasn't unusual to have armies marching through the land of those who lived on the border but it could be horrendous when these armies would often loot and set fire to buildings on their way. Other parts of England and Scotland may have been relatively calm but the Borders really suffered in Reiver times (between 1200 and 1600 approximately) when this was a wild and dangerous place.

William Wallace's army rampaged through Kielder in 1297 while Robert the Bruce is reported to have "laid waste to Keildr" in 1311/1312.

There were several settlements or villages in Kielder during medieval times. The count of Kielder, a Border Chieftain, was famous for his prowess in battle thanks to his magical armour and the mystical holly and rowan leaves he wore in his helmet. He perished suddenly during one of his many disputes and was buried in an enormous grave in Kielder.

The eerie atmosphere felt at Kielder Castle by some have scared them so badly that they headed straight for the door and refused to return. Visitors have reported hearing strange voices, heavy footsteps and seeing a shadowy figure roaming the castle.

As well as apparently being haunted by the Grey Lady, Kielder Castle's other ghostly presence is a servant girl called Emma. People have reported hearing noises in the attic room and seeing shadows in the bird room.

If nothing else, an investigation in 2009 by a team of paranormal investigators calling themselves the Grey Ladies, proved this is a haunted location that's not for the faint hearted. Noises were heard during the night from both outside and within the castle. Some were very loud yet on further investigation there was no sign of anything being disturbed. Voices and faint music was also heard during this eerie night.

In 2012 a team from Prestige Paranormal visited Kielder Castle to investigate whether or not reported ghost sightings may have some truth about them. And it did seem like there was some form of spirit presence haunting the building. During the evening, faces were seen in scrying mirrors, the shadow of a ghost named Marie was witnessed by a few people. Taps and bangs were heard in one room and a long conversation involving knocks (one for yes and two for no) was held with a ghost. A psychic contacted a grounds-man who was apparently murdered by one of the boys he'd raped in his younger days ....

Kielder Castle is now the Forestry Commission's Information Centre

Chillingham Castle: the Most Haunted Location in England

It would seem careless, when talking about haunted castles in Northumberland not to mention Chillingham (also covered in Part I of this book) and the many paranormal investigations that have been carried out in what has been described as the most haunted place in England. The castle has a gruesome history when as well as providing shelter for English soldiers it has been used as a prison for Scottish rebels. Built in the 12th century, as a monastery, it became one of the most important strongholds on the border. It was raided so regularly that it was upgraded from a stronghold to a castle in 1344.

King Edward stayed at Chillingham in 1298 on his way to battle against William Wallace and eight knights of the Garter were executed for high treason at Chillingham.

Shadows and ghostly figures that do not have a scientific explanation have appeared on photographs taken by investigators within the walls of this haunted building. It is said that a young boy who was bricked up in the Pink room can be heard screaming and trying to scratch his way out. The castle is also felt to be haunted by Lady Mary Berkely, whose husband left her alone with their baby in this huge property, after running off with her sister. When Lady Mary visits, her dress can be heard rustling as she walks and the temperature will drop suddenly, announcing her presence.

The castle's torturer, John Sage who it is believed tortured up to fifty enemies a week is said to haunt the building. As well as being able to recognise the sound of him coming as he drags his mutilated leg, he is also accompanied by a disgusting smell. It is said that John Sage strangled his lover, Elizabeth Charlton on the torture rack that is now in the torture room (not the original torture chamber of the castle which is elsewhere). Her father was a Border Reiver who insisted that Sage be put to death.

John Sage was hanged from a tree in the grounds of Chillingham Castle. Some say his dismembered body was buried at a crossroads so his ghost wouldn't know the way to heaven.

Not surprisingly, Chillingham Castle has featured on Most Haunted, Ghosthunters International and The Worlds' Scariest Places. Many paranormal investigations have been carried out here over the years

Culzean Castle Ghosts

This magnificent castle standing majestically on the Aryshire coast seems like a perfect setting for ghosts and for the eager ghost-hunter, Culzean does not disappoint. A ghostly piper is said to haunt the castle grounds, appearing in particular, to celebrate weddings of family members by serenading them with traditional Scottish tunes. His ghostly pipes can also be heard on stormy nights, the music blending eerily with the howling wind and crashing waves.

On a number of occasions in days gone by, servants of the castle have reported seeing a shadowy figure in the dungeons. It is thought that this may be the ghost of the piper who is believed to be a member of the Kennedy family who was murdered at the castle.

Here's a place where vulnerable women have been known to get their revenge on men with dishonourable intentions. Tales passed down through the ages about females associated with the castle include that of a supernatural knight who abducted a young girl and held her captive within Culzean's magnificent walls. One night, after lulling the knight to sleep, the girl stabbed him to death and escaped. Another villain, Sir John Cathcart was reputedly pushed off a cliff to his death by May Kennedy from Culzean after he abducted her from the castle. It is said that Sir Cathcart murdered his wife and was planning to murder May Kennedy. When she was warned of this she managed to kill him first and to this day he is said to haunt the ruins of Carelton Castle.

A resident ghost of Culzean is that of a woman dressed in a ball gown. Tourists have also reported seeing a peculiar misty shape moving up the oval staircase. This has been seen by a number of people and is thought to be the ghost of one of the Kennedy Clan, the original owners of the building.

The most gory story associated with Culzean occurred In the late 1500s. This is when a Kennedy from Culzean Castle had a member of the Stuart Clan seized and taken to the Black Vault in the castle. Here he was stripped naked and bound to a spit before being taken to be roasted in front of a fire. Apparently this torture was to coax Alan Stuart to sign a document that would hand his lands over to the Earl of Cassillie. Stuart was taken off the spit but six days later it is said he was forced to sign a confirmation document by being roasted again.

Since that time, visitors to the castle have heard a crackling and roaring sound of a fire accompanied by painful screams coming from within its walls.

The Most Haunted team experienced some interesting supernatural activity while visiting the castle. Other paranormal investigators have captured strange lights seen in the Earl's bedroom, on video and strange, whispering voices were recorded from the same room. Their equipment recorded sharp temperature fluctuations. A ghostly voice was recorded in the State Room and light anomalies photographed in the kitchen. Psychics have picked up on ghosts throughout the castle and lights have been seen by both visitors and paranormal investigators in one of the reception rooms downstairs. A report on one of the many investigations having been carried out at Culzean can be seen on the Ghost Finders Scotland web site.

Ghost hunting has become serious business now with many paranormal associations offering spooky evenings, ghost hunt suppers, ghost walks, paranormal nights and overnight ghost hunts. During these events there is often a medium present to help facilitate spirit communication and serious technical equipment to record possible paranormal activity. Because of the nature of the experience it can be intensely scary and most investigations are conducted to ensure those taking part get some value from the experience.

How to tell if your house is haunted

Is your house haunted? Or is it because of its history or tales you've heard about the area mixed with your over-active imagination that makes you think you're experiencing paranormal activity within your home?

There are many different types of hauntings including seeing ghosts, hearing strange sounds, sensing a presence that cannot be seen or smells that seem to come from nowhere. Objects might be seen to move by themselves or may have been moved from the place where you last left them. Often there is an explanation for what first seems to be a supernatural experience and this is what you should look for first.

Some of the most common haunted house experiences include hearing footsteps, knocks, bangs or scratching noises when no-one is there. Doors leading to rooms or doors on cupboards and cabinets might open or close by themselves. The television may switch on or off or change channels by itself or a radio might suddenly switch on. Lights might turn off and on or bulbs explode.

You might see a strange shadow out of the corner of your eye which vanishes when you turn to look at it or you may feel as if there is another presence in the room although you are alone. Sometimes this can be accompanied by a specific aroma such as a perfume, flower, or the smell of cigar smoke.

Children and animals are particularly sensitive to ghosts and you may notice your dog or cat staring at something in the room you cannot see, or the dog might bark, or the cat hiss at an area where there is no activity. Babies and young children might stare at an unseen presence and toddlers might be heard talking to a companion that only they can see and hear.

Questions you should consider if you think your house is haunted are:

1. The age and history of the house or of the land on which it was built.

2. Do other people hear strange noises as well as yourself and agree they cannot be explained?

3. Do you keep losing items like your car keys or pieces of jewellery only to have them turn up later in a place you never left them?

4. Do pets avoid some rooms of your house or act strangely in certain areas?

5. Do you feel there is someone with you although you are alone?

6. Have you noticed strange aromas such as a perfume, flowers, food, or the smell of a cigar that cannot be explained?

7. Do the lights flicker or have they switched on or off by themselves?

8. Whenever a clock stops is it always at the same time?

9. Do you often see shadowy figures out of the corner of your eye or maybe you've seen a ghost who has looked very real to you?

The above are the most common signs that a house is haunted but remember there are often explanations. We live in a very old house and our dog, for instance, would often bark at night while in the living room, for no apparent reason. It took a while to realise she was spooked by reflections and movement in the window when it was dark inside.

Explanations for doors opening or closing by themselves could be a draught coming through the house. While those scratching sounds heard in a wall could be mice, which again, hasn't been unknown in our house!

If you think your house is haunted, you might think about starting a journal to outline exactly when paranormal activity occurred and what it was. Try to capture some evidence. You might do this by using a camera or video recorder. A good analogue tape recorder might capture ghostly voices while it is possible to purchase an Electro Magnetic Frequency Detector off the internet to detect high frequency signals.

If your home is haunted and this bothers you, there are now hundreds of paranormal organisations in the UK and many other countries. You might contact a one near you for advice.

If your home is haunted and you would prefer to be left alone, stay in control. Don't let the ghost feed on your fear. Tell them firmly that this is your home and you are asking them to leave. Sometimes ghosts don't realise they are dead and they need to have this pointed out to them. Tell them that they have moved on to another spiritual plane, that you live in this house now and encourage them to follow the light.

Burning sage, spreading salt on the window sills and placing garlic in each room are all believed to ward off ghosts.

To protect yourself and your home, before going to sleep every night, visualise a bright white light surrounding you and filling every room of your home.

Real Ghost Stories Part (iv)
True Ghost and Paranormal Stories

Acknowledgements

For this section of my book, I would like to extend my sincerest thanks to all who contributed stories to this collection which would not have been possible without them. Events in this book are based on fact. Some names have been changed to protect the privacy of individuals

Introduction

Living in an old farmhouse which is haunted by at least three ghosts, according to a visiting medium and having been a psychic astrologer for over three decades, it was only a matter of time before my research took me into the realm of real hauntings. Since delving into some amazing tales of the supernatural, many of which were witnessed by several people (including accounts of highly respected police officers or members of the clergy), it is the most convincing ones I have chosen to share in this book. Some reveal fascinating legends of times gone by, some have never been published and most of these tales occur in England although examples of similar experiences are occasionally drawn from elsewhere in the world. Whether you believe in ghosts or not, these ghost stories are guaranteed to capture your imagination.

Ghost in a Cake Shop

(10th Avenue Cakes, Seaton Delaval. Photo: D Lord)

10th Avenue Cakes in Seaton Delaval, Northumberland, England looks like the most unlikely venue for a haunting. There's nothing ghoulish about the delicious cup-cakes that are served in the shop but the building itself has its eerie spots. After opening the cake shop for his daughter, Dennis wasn't particularly surprised by the number of customers who visited that would ask about their resident ghost. The family had already noticed the strange atmosphere in parts of the shop and had had their own supernatural incidents taking place in the property.

It was the back of the shop that Dennis directed me to on my visit. Despite the room being adjacent to the kitchen with the hot oven standing next to it, there was an icy feel to the tiny closet and an eerie sensation of someone watching and waiting.

Dennis has heard several reports of ghostly sightings both in and outside his shop. Taking me outside, there is an ancient wall adjacent to the building that has stood for hundreds of years. This wall is in line with the haunted closet and it is here that a dark figure clad in a long flowing robe has been seen walking quickly through the wall and away from the building.

The eerie entity is believed to be a Monk and after listening to the ghostly experiences visitors have eagerly shared from over the years, Dennis did his own research. All ghost sightings spoke of a Monk either in, leaving or entering the cake shop and ironically, it is food that lies at the root of this haunting which has links to the legend of the Monks' Stone near Tynemouth Priory.

Dennis discovered that the Monk who is believed to haunt the property is from Tynemouth. According to the legend which is likely to be true, the Monk is said to have visited a home in Seaton Delaval one day. At the time of his visit, among other savoury delights being prepared, a pig was roasting in the kitchen. The smell of cooking will have dominated the room. There will have been pots, dishes and other tools scattered around; mortar and pestle to grind herbs and spices, cooked vegetables and meat; strainers, sieves and colanders to filter liquids or foods ground in the mortar and knives to carve, bone and chop the meat. It would have been easy therefore for a Monk with a rumbling stomach on seeing a hog roasting and knives within reach to impulsively plan his next move.

No-one is certain as to the motive of the Monk for his next deed. He may have thought he wasn't doing any harm in wanting to take the head of the pig or maybe he just wanted to take something useful back for the prior's table, six miles away. After all, a pig's head could be used to make preserved jelly, Liver or black pudding.

Maybe it was the savoury smell of the roasting pig that was just too much to ignore and the poor man was hungry. Whatever the reason, the Monk hung around long enough to wait for the cook's back to be turned and much to the chagrin of the servants he quickly cut off the head, put it in his bag and carried it off in triumph, his intention being to return to Tynemouth.

The servants were reluctant to use force against a holy man to get him to return the pig but when the hot-tempered Lord of Delaval returned from hunting with his friends to find that a part of his dinner was gone, he remounted his horse in anger and rode towards Tynemouth.

The Monk was about two miles from the monastery and was taking a rest, when Lord Delaval caught up with him. The remains of a stone in a garden in Monkseaton are said to mark the spot where the Monk rested.

Lord Delaval was so furious by the Monk's deed that he beat him so hard the Monk had to crawl on hands and knees back to the monastery. He could not make it all the way and the brethren who went out in search for him found him half dead. They carried him back to the Priory but the poor man died in his cell. Because the death took place within a year and a day of the beating, Delaval was charged by the Monks of the Monastery, with his murder.

Contention in those times between the spiritual lords and temporal lords was often intense. The Church had a lot of power and even the boldest spirits, it is said, would have to bend before the power of the Church. The spiritual lords were not pleased and young Delaval was forced to make amends for what was believed to be the murder of the Monk.

As a forfeit and to receive absolution he was obliged to gift some of his lands to the monastery. These included the Manor of Elsig near Newcastle (which became a summer residence for the Priors of Tynemouth) and a good percentage of

Tynemouth. He was also ordered to set up a cross which would be known as the Rode Stane, in expiation of his violence. The Monks' Stone near the Priory remains for people to ponder on the danger of allowing temper to get the better of a man. At the base of the stone are the words: "O horrid dede, To kill a man for a pigg's hede."

Could the ghost that haunts the cake shop in Seaton Delaval be the Monk who suffered such painful consequences for stealing a pig's head? Could the building, as believed by many visitors, be the kitchen from which the deed originated? The tale itself is a true one. The Monks Stone, a sandstone obelisk (the remains of an ancient cross) was long since removed from the actual place where it was erected and now stands in the grounds of Tynemouth Priory. The exact location of the sandstone pillar is unconfirmed. The original purpose of the pillar may have been to mark the boundary assigned to the monastery of Tynemouth after Delaval was forced to sign over a portion of his land to the Church. Other theories suggest it may have been a rood-stone or market-stone around which fairs were held in olden times.

There have been many reports of paranormal activity at Tynemouth Priory including many sightings of what has been called the 'Monk Ghosts'. Strangely, many people have witnessed ghostly Monks praying (on hands and knees) in front of the stone. They have been described as wearing long brown gowns with gold/yellow rope belts and with gold markings on their hoods. Could the ghostly Monk at the Cake Shop in Seaton Delaval be one of the ghostly Monks that also haunt the Monk Stone at Tynemouth Priory?

(Since the above was written, the Cake Shop has closed and the building is used for different purposes).

There are many tales of hauntings at Tynemouth Priory but not so well known, are the stories linked with the mysterious cave below the Priory where infernal spirits are said to dwell and the tales of fairies that are believed to have lived on the coast at Tynemouth.

Because of a series of landslides, the cave entrance collapsed and was closed for good and there are no signs now of an entrance but in the late 1880s the cave was accessible to the public. The cave was known to locals as Geordie's Hole or Jingler's Hole. Some thought it may have been a part of an underground passage with vaults and possibly dungeons connected to the priory. Other legends speak of a witch or wizard of Tynemouth having lived there. Another tale tells of an old man who lived in the cave below the Priory who used to prowl around at night making strange clanking noises that terrified local children.

According to an article in the Monthly Chronicle written in 1887, Tynemouth was a favourite haunt of the fairies. An old woman who was visited by one of the article writer's friends could recollect stories about fairies going back at least fifty years and the woman herself spoke of having seen fairies when she was a girl.

The Two Soldiers

As told by Lorna Webb:

"My grandmother lived in a town called Johnstone. It was built to ease the Glasgow overspill and lies 12 miles west of Glasgow City. It was predominately built to house the people of Glasgow who had lost their homes due to bombing during the war. Many families were displaced and there was also the need for more housing for workers in the main industries at that time: the Cotton and Thread Industries. A castle built in 1771 once stood here and was remodelled in 1812 by George Houstoun. It is said that the castle was visited by the Polish composer Chopin in 1848. He spent time here convalescing after a near fatal accident while out riding in a two horse carriage.

Much of Johnstone Castle was demolished by 1950 and all that remains today is the central square tower along with a crow-stepped bartizaned section of an older date. The tower is protected as category B listed building. It was bought by the local council and work began shortly afterwards. Council houses were built around the remains of the castle.

During the war parts of the castle and grounds were used as an official German prisoner of war camp: Working camp No. 188. The camp was comprised of corrugated iron huts initially used for Polish soldiers. Additions were made to the camp following the Clydebank Blitz. These photos show what remains of this castle.

I was sitting with my Grandmother, one day, chatting about the castle. She had a perfect view of it from her bedroom window. She casually told me that she had experienced a few visits from men in uniform. She would tell me that she didn't think they fought in the same regiment. I asked her how she knew all this (my Grandmother was Clairvoyant) and she went on to explain that one man was in an olive green uniform and the other was in a grey uniform. She saw them quite regularly. The first time she saw them, she was collecting laundry to be done. As she carried her laundry basket downstairs she watched as a man in a green uniform walked out her kitchen, through the hall and into her living room. She was the only one home that day. This was long after the War, in the 1960's. She walked into her living room and there was no-one there. Yet he had been as clear as day and very solid looking. This continued on a regular basis and he always walked the same route through my Granny's house. One day he stopped in the hall, turned to face my Grandmother and nodded at her while touching his cap. My Grandmother explained that she nodded back and sent him healing and love.

A soldier in a grey uniform soon started to use my Granny's house as a shortcut to somewhere. She would regularly see both of them going about their ways and always disappearing through a brick wall. - I was completely mesmerised when she told me these stories.

I asked her why she wasn't scared. I always remember her words to this day. She said to me "Lorna, never be scared of the dead. They will never hurt you; only the living". Never a truer word was spoken.

My Granny explained that in the 60's she had a huge boulder in her garden which made it difficult to cut around the grass. She had asked the local council if they could come out and remove the huge stone. It was far too heavy for one and even two men to move. It required something much stronger. She told me that she long suspected that one or both of these soldiers were buried somewhere close to the house. There is no cemetery there (current day) in relation to the war as far as I am aware.

Gran explained that she needed to know, and the only way was to ask the local council to remove the stone. The Council came out to inspect this large boulder. After digging around for a while they realised they had found something. It appeared to be a polish button from an army uniform. There was also some sort of artefact that they suspected had come from a cap. My Grandmother promptly asked the workmen to put the stone back. She told them it was there for good reason. The workmen duly did this. My Grandmother asked the local priest to come and bless the ground, in memory of all the soldiers that had bravely lost their lives while fighting for their countries. He did!

She never saw the soldiers again."

Are 'Ghosts' real? - You bet your ACTUAL life they are!

As told by Lorna Webb:

"I was sound asleep when I heard her calling me. "Lorna!" "Lorna, you need to get up." She was saying it over and over to me. My brain started to rouse. I was finding it so hard to wake up being in such a deep sleep. It was nearly 4 am. "Lorna, you need to get up now pet." – I could hear the urgency in my Granny's voice. I duly did as I was told. As I opened my eyes I could not focus. I waited for my eyes to adjust but still I could not see.

I started to choke and my eyes started to sting. "Why can I not see?" I wondered. I made my way in the dark to my bedroom light. I switched it on and I still could not see a thing. I switched it back off and stood there wondering what on earth was going on. I felt wave of panic creep in. I opened my bedroom door and was blown backward onto my bed with the whoosh of smoke and energy.

I regained my balance and got up to slam my door shut. I had no idea what was going on but knew that I had to get my family out of the house. My younger brother and sister were in another room. So was my mother. My father was working night shift that night. I couldn't get out of my room because of the smoke, the heat was so intense. My lungs filled with smoke as I shouted over and over for my mum. She couldn't hear me. I wondered how I could get her attention. I screamed out loud a curdling "Mum!" I heard two quick thuds as her feet hit her bedroom floor. We had to feel our way out of the house. We could not even see our hand in front of our faces. We all managed to get out the house that night. As we sat next door getting over the shock of our house fire, a Senior Fire Officer asked if he could have a private word with me.

He went on to explain that during 3am and 4am we are in the deepest of sleeps. The fire had come into contact with a large bottle of liquid which was used to boost fire in outdoor BBQ's. This had set our whole kitchen on fire and it had spread fast. He explained that it was the smoke that was deadlier than the flames due to the toxins. He asked me what had woken me up (this was before the days of smoke alarms). I told him I could hear things melting and falling from a height onto the floor. – He was a man of science. How on earth could I possibly tell him that my Grandmother had woken me? She had passed away 11 months before!"

Matthew

As told by Lorna Webb:

I was sitting chatting with my cousin, catching up with the past week events. Cheryl's kids were at school and nursery so we had the morning to ourselves. She was telling me that she had a dream about Matthew her friend. In her dream Matthew had told her that he was all right now and he could walk about no problem. He was running about and all excited because he was 'normal' again and pain free.

Matthew was a childhood friend of my cousin. They went to school together and played together at home as they lived close. Matthew became unwell and it was soon after this he was diagnosed with Motor Neuron Disease. A few years after this he became reliant on a wheel chair with minimum movement capabilities.

Cheryl would go round after school to help out with his care. She carried on doing this until she became a mother herself. Cheryl left the town to raise her children and as her family expanded she found it difficult to continue to see Matthew. It had been a few years since she had seen Matthew but they did keep in touch via mobile phone on occasion.

During our chat, Cheryl told me that she would need to phone Matthew as she was a bit concerned that something was wrong. Cheryl received a phone call the following day to say that Matthew had passed away. She was so upset, feeling that she had let Matthew down in some way. I tried to reassure her that the visit from him in her dream was to let her know that he is perfectly well now and that he made it do the other side safely. She was to take comfort in this.

The following week we were catching up as usual. I left the room to go to the backroom and was overwhelmed by the smell of aftershave as I went upstairs. There was no-one else in the house at the time. Cheryl is single and lives with her four children. Her children were at school and nursery. I felt a cold draft and got Goosebumps. I called Cheryl upstairs to see if she could smell it. We both have the ability for Clairalience. She could smell it too. We could both feel the breeze and could 'feel' exactly where this male energy was standing. We could smell the aftershave again!

We went back downstairs and Cheryl left the house to pick up Ciara from nursery. When she came back we poured a fresh cup of tea as Ciara pottered between her toys upstairs and watched CBeebies. As we were talking I felt an energy walk past me and so did Cheryl. We decided to meditate and pray for a while and as we were doing so we could hear Ciara laughing really hard. We could hear her talking to someone. Ciara was born In Caulk and is a Rainbow child. Her abilities are very sharp and she is encouraged to talk freely and express herself. Ciara is four years old.

We called her in and asked her who she was talking to. Ciara replied "Matthew"! We were gobsmacked. Ciara had never met Matthew. Cheryl did not discuss Matthew with her children. We asked her who Matthew was and sat and watched her ask out loud, to the air, "who are you?" She replied "He says he is mummy's friend." She kept telling us how funny he was and that he was making her laugh. She told us that he kept making funny faces at her. We sat intrigued to say the very least watching her converse with someone who wasn't visible to the naked eye.

Cheryl and Ciara continued to receive messages from Matthew for a few weeks after that. He asked Cheryl to pass on some messages to his family which she duly respected and did so. Matthew hasn't been around for a while now. I guess that's because he is in a good place now."

The Ghost of Anne Frank

As told by Dennis Lord:

"It might sound like a strange place for this story to be told for I live in a very nice town on the North East coast of England. I was born in this fishing port with its miles of golden beach where I learned to swim as a little boy.

I spent all my young life here, was married here, had two children here ... then lost my wife of forty years on Christmas day 2011.

We had married ten days after we met her on the seafront at a little fishing village up the coast from North Shields called Cullercoats and this is where we lived most of our married life with our children.

Well, North Shields is also a sea port, with ferries to many places but in later years, a daily ferry to Amsterdam with very cheap fares. My wife, daughter and I used to go many times a year. They loved the Bulb fields and Flower Markets and shops.

So I was left to my own devices when we were in Amsterdam. They would often leave the hotel early to do the

Flower Markets and shops and I got to know Amsterdam very well over the years. I would do all the local sightseeing things – there are only so many times you can go around the Red Light District! I got to know a lot of the Local Bar Owners, my favourite being Louis Bar, just off Dam Square. I am not a great drinker, so I used to sit by the Canals and watch the world go by. – I can recommend Amsterdam for the place to people watch.

I had been going to Amsterdam since the 1960s when it was a lot less busy so I had visited the art galleries and museums when they were a lot quieter. I had even been to Anne Frank's house when you did not have to queue – spent lots of time there, listened to all the stories of Anne and her family and how they had gone into hiding from the Germans after they'd left Germany to live a safer life in Holland. But it was not to be as the Germans invaded Holland and started to persecute the Jews living there, eventually deporting them to the Death Camps. Anne and her family had felt safe in Holland and had a good life 'til they heard about how Margot, Anne's sister had been called up to the Deporting Centre. So the whole family had gone into hiding. Anne's father Otto, her mother, Edith, sister Margo and another family, Mr and Mrs Van Pels with their son Peter (who Anne fell in love with). It must have been very hard for seven strangers to live together. Then, later another man came to live there. They were supplied with food and other things through friends who put themselves in great danger by helping the hidden families. So, that was Anne's life and you can read it all in depth in many books: The Diary of Anne Frank, The Story of Anne Frank and many more.

So, during my stays in Amsterdam, I would wander around the town, stop at café's and bars or just sit by the Canal and read.

Many times I sat outside the Anne Frank Museum and house and watched the crowds of people going in from all over the world. I think I was hoping the crowds would get smaller so I could go in and have a look at the changes they'd made, since I was there in the '60s, but it was always busy from first thing in the morning 'til it closed.

Well, I have told you I am a great people watcher. I would try and guess where people came from by how they were dressed and as you can guess there were many young people who I would think had read Anne's diary.

Called the Diary of a Young Girl and translated into every language in the world, I think I was probably the only person in the world who had never read it. But I used to think of Anne a lot and what her family went through. I had seen the film about her story, read little bits about her life and still I had never read her diary. Don't ask me why. I just feel I do not need to, after meeting Anne. "Meeting Anne?" you are going to say "But she died just before the end of the War!" And, I was not born until 1950, but yes, I believe I met Anne Frank.

So, let me tell you this little story: One day, sitting in my usual place on a lovely Dutch morning (and those of you who have been to Amsterdam will know what I mean). I can't explain it but it is an Amsterdam thing: the hustle and bustle of a big city, the sunlight coming through the buildings and trees, both of which are very big along the Canals; the boats with sightseers, working boats, houseboats so different o any place on earth! People were going about their daily business, the shops on both banks of the Canal opening for trade, the young ladies of the Red Light District going home after a busy night, the older ones on their way to do the day shift. If you have been down the Red Light District you will know what I mean. Everyone passing greetings in Dutch and English – most people in Holland speak English which is good for me as

I only speak English and Geordie at that. Well, as I was saying, I was sitting by the Canal in front of Anne Frank's House Museum, eating ice-cream (I love ice-cream. Wherever I go I have to have an ice-cream at least once a day!).

So here I am, sitting watching all the people going by. It was very busy as I have said, then along comes a young lady. Do not ask me why I should think her strange but something made me notice her. The clothes she wore for instance were not modern. You still see people in National Costume all over Holland but it was not that. These seemed very dated. As she came up to me she spoke to me in German and that had never happened before in Holland. She said "Guten Morgen mein herr," then the strangest thing ever, I said "Guten Morgen, Fraulein." Well as I told you before I only speak English with a Geordie accent and a very strong one so I have been told.

But the funny thing is, it just came straight out. Well what can I say about this young lady? She was in her early teens, very striking features and very dark smiley eyes. I must admit it did not frighten me but made me focus if that this the right word. When I had time to think, she was gone. Strange but it never occurred to me that this was anyone special. But what happened next was even stranger. I found myself drawn to the same spot every day. I never told my wife and daughter. I just got up and ready and went for my walk but I ended up the same place every day. I was just drawn to go there and it felt weirdly natural to me. I didn't question why. And when there, I just sat and people watched as I had always done.

Our break in Amsterdam finished and we went home to our little village Cullercoats and settled into everyday life but it was not long before my wife decided that she and our daughter were going back to Amsterdam and did I want to go?

I replied "No thanks I will give it a miss this time," but as the time got closer for them to go I started to have sleepless nights thinking about the strange young lady I had seen. I don't know why but I told my wife I had changed my mind as there were a few more things I would like to see in Amsterdam, I never told them of my encounter.

So we arrived in Amsterdam. I couldn't wait to get the suitcases in the hotel and be out in the streets. It was late summer but dry and nice to enjoy walking the canals. Then, I ended up in my usual place at the Anne Frank House, not sure what I was hoping to see. But it was just the usual assortment of tourists, a lot older this time. I think the schools had gone back but still large crowds queuing to get in. I did think I would join the queue but I knew it had all changed and you could only look at the House though glass screens – when I had gone in the 60s you could walk in the house.

Every day during that stay I would go for walks in different directions but would still end up in front of Anne's house. I'm not sure why but I was starting to feel really down. We were going home late the next day and I knew on the last day I was expected to go shopping with the family.

That next day I awoke early left a note for my wife saying I could not sleep so I was going for a walk. I think my idea was to get to the front of the queue at Anne Frank's House. But when I got there it was first light and there was nobody around. So I called at a Baker's got a pastry and a carton of milk and sat down to wait for the crowds to appear.

I was just daydreaming and looked up and suddenly the strange lady was standing in front of me. She said, "Hello."

I replied, "I thought you were German?"'.

She told me she was, but had come to live in Amsterdam after the Germans started persecuting the Jews before the War started.

She said she came to Amsterdam with her mother, father and sister and that they had lived in that house for two years. Her family were in hiding in the attic with another family and a dentist came later who she did not like. She fell in love with the other family's son called Peter.

We talked about everyday things. I told her about my wife and family and where I came from. – Now all of this was in perfect English which didn't seem strange to me.

She told me her name was Anna, she did not say Anne. She told me how happy she was that children from all over the world came to see the house and that they had read her diary. She asked if I had read it. I admitted I hadn't and she smiled and said that I would one day.

She mentioned how they were betrayed by a friend of the family and told me his name. She said she forgave him and she was with all her family and friends. Then the young lady stood up saying "I must go as people will be coming to see the House." Before she left, she told me to enjoy life and not to worry as "everything comes good in the end."

And that is how I met Anne Frank."

Haunted Roads in England

Many years ago before the M20 was complete, a man called Andrew set off from Dover to travel to Southampton. He was using the coast road and on one stretch of the A259 near Bexhill, his car engine suddenly stopped and the car rolled to a silent halt. This occurred late at night so in the darkness with all the lights of the car just suddenly going out and with Andrew being a laid-back young man, the experience seemed more scary than eerie.

All of a sudden everything had become deadly silent. Andrew was in the middle of nowhere and his car, for no apparent reason, had just died. As well as the car having slowed to a stop, there was no electrical power.

Automatically Andrew tried turning the key but there was nothing. Just that worrying click, click that suggested he had a dead battery. There were no other cars around, it was a moonless night and Andrew could see nothing but blackness when he looked outside. He did not have a mobile phone, something so often taken for granted nowadays, so he had no way to contact anyone. He would just have to wait until another driver passed by.

After sitting for what felt like ages in the dark, he wasn't feeling so laid-back; panic was starting to set in. It was winter. It was cold. Without any heaters his hands and feet were starting to feel numb. He had not come prepared for anything like this and he wasn't dressed for warmth, having been relying, when he'd set off, on the warmth of his vehicle. His imagination started to work overtime. What if no-one came? How long should he wait in the cold? What if there was 'something' out there? Andrew made sure the doors of his car were locked.

Eventually ... was it panic or an increasing impatience that led him to try the key again? Whatever it was, on the first turn of the key, the engine started, the radio came on again as did the interior light and the headlights. They lit up the road ahead and Andrew thought he'd never felt so thankful.

All seemed to be working fine and he managed to drive to his destination with no further problems and an immense sense of relief. Later, on discussing his experience, it seemed all the more eerie when he discovered that other people too had undergone something very similar on that very same stretch of road.

There are a number of theories about why car engines seem to die in the same spots on the same roads when there is plenty of fuel in the tank. Some believe it may be where accidents have occurred.

For instance when Joe who isn't a religious person and neither does he believe in ghosts was driving uphill in Malta his car engine died. It started up again when he turned the key and he never gave the matter another thought until it happened again in exactly the same spot on another occasion. This time his wife was with him and as he went to turn the key she stopped him saying that they had to say a little prayer for the dead. After the prayer, Joe started the engine and drove home. He never experienced the problem again.

Witnesses who have seen UFOs while driving, often report that their car engine died just prior to or during the incident. In 2006 in Poland, while returning from a wedding party, two men spotted a silver object flying across the road. A moment later their car engine stopped, as did the engine of the car behind them. Photographs were taken of this incident which lasted around 8 minutes. In 1958, at the Loch Raven Reservoir, twenty miles from Baltimore, two men who were driving around 11 pm, were amazed to see A UFO hovering over the only narrow bridge on the road. They slowed their car down and crept up slowly to the scene. The car engine stopped. The men had nowhere to go and could only stand there watching until the object vanished and the car engine started up again. Reports were filed with the police department.

Back to England now and the ghost of a black dog has been seen to run across the A6 near Shap Fell, before it vanishes over the edge of a cliff. Also on the A6 at Barrock Hill, near Carlisle, the ghost of a highway man can occasionally be heard crying for help near the spot where he is said to have been hanged for murder. According to local legend, the rope used in the hanging was not tight enough and it took days for the man to die.

The Capon Tree ghosts haunt a road just outside Brampton. Apparently six highlanders from the Jacobite rebellion were hanged there in 1745 and on the anniversary of their hanging, the bodies of the Highlanders can sometimes be seen, swinging in the trees. In that same year, Bonnie Prince Charlie and his men stayed in a building in Brampton which is now Hamilton's Shoe Shop. Apparently this is where his army were barracked while he lay siege to the City of Carlisle.
On hearing news of the Prince's defeat, six of his supporters were hanged from a tree to the south of Brampton. A monument now stands in place of the tree, commemorating the event.

Among the many ghosts at Levens Hall in Cumbria is the Grey Lady who according to legend was a gypsy woman who laid a curse on the family of the house. The Grey Lady has appeared in front of several motorists on their approach to Levens Hall. Some reported seeing a Grey Lady standing in the road. Many had to brake suddenly or swerve to avoid hitting her yet on getting out of their cars they discovered that the ghostly figure had disappeared.

Girls and Boys come out to Play

The following ghost story is the kind that horror movies are made of only there is nothing fictional about this tale, the witnesses being highly respected police officers.

Police Officer PC Dick Ellis from South Yorkshire and a former Special Constable, John Beet, were two of a number of witnesses to a ghostly apparition on the A616 bypass near Sheffield in England, while the road was under construction.

The incident occurred on a September's night in 1987. The story goes that two security guards who were patrolling the area had phoned their boss, in a frantic state. Their boss, Peter Owens arrived at the scene to find the two men in a state of hysteria. According to the security guards strange things had started occurring around midnight the night before. They'd been driving along the road near Stocksbridge Steelworks to see children playing near the bypass some distance away from the nearest houses. The men, who deciding to investigate, parked their land rover and sat watching as the children played. Both men were puzzled by the children's old-fashioned clothing.

Concerned that children were playing out so late so far away from their homes, the men got out of their car and walked in the direction they'd seen them only to find the girls and boys had vanished. At the spot where they'd seen the children play, there were no footprints in the mud. In fact there were no signs of anyone having been there. Not particularly spooked by the strange episode, the next morning, the baffled men described their story to other workmen who confessed that they too had heard children's voices in the night as they rested in their caravans.

So how had their confusion turned into terror? What had sparked the reason for the hysterical phone call to their boss?

The security guards went on to explain how, just before they'd phoned their boss, they had been driving up Pearoyd Lane towards the construction site. As they reached the site they saw a large, dark figure of a Monk on the partly constructed bridge. Driving towards the figure, the headlights shone directly onto it and the apparition vanished.

The men were serious about their story; this was no prank and their boss decided to call the police. The amused police officer who took the call, PC Ellis suggested they call a priest instead of the police. Which is exactly what was done as either later that day or the next morning, the police officer received a phone call from a priest, Stuart Brindley! The priest asked if the station could send someone out to help him with two security guards at his church. The priest explained that the men were demanding that the partly constructed bridge be exorcised.

It was time for the police to investigate the story and PC Ellis and Special Constable John Beet went out to the site apparently quite sceptical about the supposed haunting and joking about this being the most hilarious case they'd ever had to investigate. The policemen parked their car facing the bridge with the windows down. As they observed the scene, they noticed something moving on the bridge. Ellis went up to investigate and found a piece of loose tarpaulin flapping in the wind. He could see the pylon where the security guards claimed to have seen children playing but the place was quiet and there was no-one round. The tarpaulin is what had probably spooked the security guards.

He returned to the car and they were about ready to leave when PC Ellis had an odd chilly sensation going down his spine. He then suddenly felt a presence at his side and turned his head to see a dark, clothed figure standing right next to his car door. The dark clothing had a white V shaped material running down the chest. As quickly as it appeared, the apparition vanished, appearing instantly beside John Beet's door before vanishing again. PC Ellis got out of his car and looked around and underneath the vehicle but nothing was there. Both police officers had seen a figure, there hadn't been time to for it to get away so fast without them seeing where. The situation was starting to get very eerie.

When he got back in the panda and turned the ignition nothing happened. He tried again. The car would not start. On the third attempt the engine started.

The police officers drove to away from the construction site. As they were driving they suddenly heard something hit the back of the car. PC Ellis described this as like the sound of people hitting the car with sticks and bats. They stopped the car and got out but they could see no damage. As PC Ellis reached into the car to radio the station, they heard three or four loud bangs on the back of the car. This time the vehicle rocked up and down as the booming noise reverberated around the car. Now thoroughly spooked, the men needed no further encouragement to return to the police station.

Here they reported their findings to shocked colleagues and wrote statements of their experience. Both police officers admitted their fear was so intense that it was worse than the fear of being about to encounter danger, it was the kind of fear you have absolutely no control over … a feeling of "dread."

The bypass opened on Friday 13th 1989 and paranormal activity in that area continued. The deaths of at least 24 people involved in traffic accidents on the bypass have been attributed to the alleged sightings of a ghostly Monk. However after an attempt to make the A616 bypass safer the number of serious injuries and deaths dropped considerably.

But what of the ghostly Monk who has been witnessed by so many on that road? Who might he be? A local historian suggests that this could be a Monk who, after becoming disillusioned with the harsh life at a nearby monastery, he left to work as a gardener at Underbank Hall where he remained for the rest of his life. Only because he had left the monastery the Monk was buried in unhallowed ground on a nearby hillside. This hillside had been cut through for the Stocksbridge Bypass.

According to local legend, his spirit is disquiet because his grave has been disturbed. There are also rumours that the ghostly children who are seen playing in the area may be the spirits of those who were buried alive in mining accidents or killed when a cart carrying youngsters home from a day out overturned.

Haunted A75 in Dumfries and Galloway

It was a dark, misty night in October 1958 when Hugh Watson Reid, an experienced lorry driver who lived in West Lothian was driving his articulated vehicle towards Carlisle. Hugh, a sensible man would not have described himself as being religious or imaginative. He did not believe in ghosts. Although it was misty, visibility was reasonable.

Just as he approached a left hand bend in the road at the junction with the A75 to Annan, he saw a middle-aged couple step out from the side of the road to walk in front of his lorry. As the couple who were casually walking across the road arm-in-arm were framed in his headlights, Mr Watson slammed his foot down hard on the footbrake and switched on his hazard warning lights.

The couple were dressed weirdly, as if they had been to a fancy-dress party. The man had been wearing a High Tile Hat, a short double-breasted jacket and tight trousers. The woman wore a crinoline ankle length gown and a large bonnet-type hat. They seemed to be dressed more for summer and warm weather and this was not the type of clothing that a middle-aged couple would be expected to be wearing on a cold October night in the 1950s.

The lorry stopped without him hitting the couple but angry at their carelessness, he got out of the lorry intending to point out the stupidity of wandering across a main road so late at night without looking. As he reached the front of the lorry, he realised they had vanished.

For a second Mr Watson had an awful feeling that they might be under his cabin but he checked and there was no sign of them. They weren't on the road around him or beside the lorry. There was a thick hedge that separated the road from the fields beyond, that no-one could have got through.

Disturbed by the experience he drove on to Carlisle. Some months later he discovered that he had not been the only driver to have witnessed this spooky couple's manifestation. Others, too, have had a man and woman dressed in ancient costume walk in front of their vehicle at exactly the same spot. The incident always occurs at night.

A number of ghostly incidents taking place on the A75 in Dumfries and Galloway have been reported to the police. There seems to be a ghostly car that drives the road with dipped headlights which one minute is there and then suddenly it vanishes. One family almost had a horrific accident when this phantom vehicle appeared to drive straight into them. They swerved to avoid the vehicle, their car landing in a ditch while the ghostly car just vanished.

Local police frequently received reports of people seeing a car being driven dangerously and then vanishing. They have looked for a rational explanation for the haunting but could offer nothing except that: that's what it was, a haunting. Other ghostly sightings along the same road include that of a young girl who appears without warning in front of vehicles. Drivers often think they may have hit her only to discover, once they stop and get out of their cars, that there is no sign of anyone. If that isn't all, other ghostly reports include a phantom furniture van, an old lady, and animals which fly towards vehicles then vanish.

Haunted Trains and Railway Stations

Almost every country around the world will have its railway lines and railway stations that are reputed to be haunted. Some paranormal experts suggest that a traumatic event such as a sudden unexpected death can be a catalyst for a haunting. It is also possible that the very nature of railway stations, where people meet, greet, depart, say their final goodbyes or their first 'hellos' and the intense emotion associated with these occasions could be another reason why they are associated with hauntings.

How many women have bidden a sad farewell to their soldier husbands or boyfriends as they've stepped onto a train to go off to war? How many mothers, eyes filled with tears, have waved goodbye to their soldier sons as they proudly and excitedly waited on the platform to play their part in defending their country?

Railway yards are dangerous places to work in with their network of tracks, trains being moved around, maintenance equipment, toxic substances and noisy repairs crowding the atmosphere. And in the darkness, with large shapes outlined against the evening sky, spooky sounds and eerie sensations, the atmosphere is conducive to tales of ghosts and the supernatural.

There is no building now in Addiscombe railway yard, Surrey. However before the shed was demolished, a worker in the railway yard saw an eerie figure walking from the sheds. He described the apparition as being dressed in grey with a blurred and distorted face. Other people reported having heard the distinct sound of machinery being moved at night even though the buildings were locked and there was no-one in the sheds.

The ghost of a fireman is said to haunt the sheds at the ancient railway station at Darley Dale in Derbyshire while the shadowy figure of a driver who was killed in an accident in the shed at Dunster Station in Somerset has been witnessed by several people.

Can there by ghostly trains? On the old railway track between Goldmire Junction and Millwood Junction in Dalton in Furness, Cumbria, a number of people reported hearing the whooshing sound of an engine pass them by. They even felt the rush of wind experienced as if a train was going past them yet nothing was seen. This ghostly experience involved noise and sensation yet nothing visual.

Ghost hunting tours are offered in many places in the UK and Carlisle, Cumbria is one of them. Those who enjoy being spooked say there is nothing more eerie than a tour of the Railway Station at night. During the day, the Victorian station is alive with activity but it is said that as darkness descends, there is a strange eeriness about the place. Travellers waiting for their train to arrive can feel unsettled, hearing weird sounds, seeing shadows and feeling as if they are being watched. Workers at the station have reported seeing doors opening by themselves and when double-checking, there has been no-one there.

(vintage postcard: Carlisle Railway Station c. 1950s
Copyright not stated)

A number of ghosts are said to haunt the station. Spend a while on Platform 8 and you might encounter a headless man who occasionally appears. While a woman in a veil is said to travel along the corridors underneath the station.

What many people don't realise is that underneath the station lies a labyrinth of rooms connected by stone corridors known as the Undercroft. These rooms have had various uses over the years and according to Census records, people in the late 1800s resided in the station. Some were born, lived and died there. Among the rooms there is an old buffet room, a lamp room where young boys were employed to keep paraffin lamps filled, a locker room, staff accommodation, a cold store and a butcher's room. Regular ghost-hunts are arranged at the station and spiritual tools used during these investigations include pendulums, glass work, spirit boards and scientific equipment such as thermometers and EMF readers.

A check of census records also shows that Carlisle Railway Station provided jobs for many people living in the area in the late 1800s. Among some of the people working there included 39 year old Henry Foster who lived in Shields Court. He was a

Lampman. 30 year old Robert Barclay was a Railway Stoker as was 25 year old James Franklin (who lived in Princess Street). 34 year old John (jnr) Blenkisopp who lived At Halfway Houses was a Railway Yardsman while 24 yr old Henry Bulman who was a boarder in Grey street was a Railway Shunter (pointsman). 29 year old William Carrick was a Railway Engine Fireman while 17 year old James Swan Harvey was a Railway Clerk. These were real people who may have spent a good percentage of their life at Carlisle Railway Station, sharing their highs and lows and even perhaps, while eating their bait, sharing their own ghost stories.

Those who have been on these tours enjoyed the experience but felt that smaller groups would have allowed them a better chance to soak in the atmosphere.

Haunted Carlisle

(Carlisle Vintage postcard published by Valentines (no longer trading))

One of the most haunted places by far in Carlisle is the Castle. Standing near the border of England and Scotland, Carlisle Castle has a long and gruesome history. The Castle is now a military headquarters to a Royal Regiment and up until recent years, a part of this building was used to house Carlisle Archive Centre.

Over the years there have been many ghost stories told by visitors, workers and soldiers stationed at the Castle. In the 1830s, during some demolition work prior to building a new barracks and parade ground, a workman found the skeleton of a lady bricked up in the staircase in the Captain's Tower. She had been wearing a silk, tartan dress when she died and there were three rings on her fingers. She was holding a young child. There were no records to give a hint of why this woman and child might have been there and some believe she lived in Elizabethan times and was walled in, alive.

Since the discovery of her skeleton, a ghostly woman has been seen at the castle. A sentry on guard duty in 1842 saw a figure of a woman approaching him in the early hours of the morning. He challenged her to stop but she ignored him. He shouted to alert the other guardsman and then raising his bayonet, charged at the figure. The moment he reached her, the woman vanished into thin air. According to some reports, the soldier got such a shock he collapsed to the ground in a faint. Although his fellow guardsmen managed to rouse him and he told them what happened, the experience petrified him and within moments he died … he had literally been scared to death.

Visitors cannot help but feel chilled by the many tales of hauntings at the Castle. Included in its long list of ghosts is the spectre that haunts the Half Moon Battery, the two medieval soldiers who have been seen on the top floor of the castle keep and a ghostly sentry who sits inside the archway of the inner keep. Apparently the ghost who has been seen leaning against the wall in the upper keep is that of King Stephen. Some visitors have witnessed a ghost who appeared so real they did not realise until later that they'd had a supernatural experience. This is the yeoman dressed in period clothes who walks up and down the path running in front of the cellblock towards the old Regimental Headquarters. Many mistake him as being someone in costume until they hear he is a well-known ghost in that area.

As a serving soldier of the Border Regiment, Frederick Graham recounted the Christmas of 1954 when he was sleeping alone on the ground floor of the Arroyo Billet. During the night he was attacked by a ghost who seemed intent on strangling him. Frederick said that it was the most horrific night of his life.

(Carlisle Castle, 2012)

Mary, Queen of Scots was incarcerated in Carlisle Castle in 1568. Fleeing from her subjects in a small fishing boat, she arrived in Workington and was escorted, with due respect and courtesy, to Cockermouth Castle. From there she was escorted to Carlisle Castle where she was housed in modest quarters.

Although she was allowed to wander around the castle, hospitality soon became imprisonment. Disappointed with the clothing Elizabeth supplied for her and much to the unease of Francis Knolly who was there to keep watch over her, she began to order grand clothes from Edinburgh. – Clothes for which Elizabeth had to pay. The captive Queen was allowed to walk the terrace of the outer ward of the castle. She attended Sunday service in Carlisle

Cathedral and occasionally would stroll the banks of the Eden with her ladies.

Apparently she was also allowed to join in some of the hunts much to the chagrin of her warders who worried that she would take advantage of being on horseback to gallop back to Scotland. Some say that the ghostly spirit of her custodian Sir Francis Knolly still haunts the castle. Although Queen Mary's ghost haunts many places and royal households in the UK, she has not been seen at Carlisle Castle. According to John Robson on a guided tour of Carlisle's haunted houses, her ghost has been seen in Long Lane.

In 1992, alarms at the castles King's Own Border Regiment museum were set off for three nights in a row. The culprit was never found but rumour has it that an apparition seen to be gliding under an arch between the exhibition and the gift shop area was to blame.

The Cursing Stone –
Can a whole City be cursed?

A stone which has been inscribed by an ancient curse is now housed at Tully House museum in Carlisle. Although commissioned to mark the millennium, many now call it the Cursing Stone, blaming it for the cloud of misfortune that seems to have hung over the city since it was installed in the museum in 2001.

The curse referred to on the stone is over 500 years old and was made by a man of the cloth. Angry and dismayed by the havoc and mayhem caused by the Border Reivers on all those who lived on or near the border of England and Scotland, the Archbishop of Glasgow issued a venomous curse against the Reivers.

More than 1000 words long it has been called the 'mother of all curses.' This magnificent diatribe was delivered from every pulpit throughout the Borders. Church-goers may have been stunned by its venom and its length but it held no sway over the Reivers who were merely amused by the Archbishop's ranting.

The massive stone was housed at the museum just over ten years ago and the artist who designed the stone took 300 words of the curse made in 1525. The stone, costing £10,000 was commissioned to mark Carlisle's Millennium Gateway Scheme. Ever since, the inhabitants of Carlisle have experienced a string of disastrous events which some blame on the curse. These include: an outbreak of foot and mouth disease (which was also experienced throughout the UK), local factories closing down and jobs lost and Carlisle United football team kept losing games. In early 2005 Carlisle suffered flooding of which no-one alive had witnessed before. Houses on the main roads leading into town were flooded as were many in the town centre itself. Ten years later, unbelievably, Carlisle was hit again by severe flooding from the River Eden. Streets and streets of houses looked more like rivers, bridges were damaged, supermarkets and businesses destroyed and schools closed.

Some inhabitants of Carlisle, having noticed much of the misfortune that had plagued the city had occurred since the stone was housed at Tully House, began calling it the Cursing Stone; a name which has stuck.

People from the church held debates to consider whether the curse on the stone could be the cause of so much ill fortune. Councillor Jim Tootle who has also blamed the Cursing Stone for the food-and-mouth outbreak and floods in which three local people perished, asked for the stone to be removed and destroyed. His request was turned down. Sadly, the councillor died in November 2011 after a sudden illness.

He had a reputation for always speaking out on behalf of the people who had contacted him. Many had approached him feeling anxious about the Cursing Stone and this is why he had insisted that the curse should be taken seriously.

The curse was aimed at the Reivers who flouted the law, stole cattle, destroyed crops, burned homes and murdered. People from all walks of life were drawn into reiving; their descendants continue to live in the Carlisle area and can be found all over the world today. The curse was vivid in its intentions:

I curse their head and all the hairs of their head; I curse their face, their brain, their mouth, their nose, their tongue, their teeth, their forehead, their shoulders, their breast, their heart, their stomach, their back, their womb, their arms, their leggs, their hands, their feet, and every part of their body, from the top of their head to the soles of their feet, before and behind, within and without.

The Archbishop's mind must have been working overtime as he wrote this, making certain no area of their life was free from this jinx:

I curse them going and I curse them riding; I curse them standing and I curse them sitting; I curse them eating and I curse them drinking; I curse them rising, and I curse them lying; I curse them at home, I curse them away from home; I curse them within the house, I curse them outside of the house; I curse their wives, their children, and their servants who participate in their deeds; their crops, their cattle, their wool, their sheep, their horses, their swine, their geese, their hens, and all their livestock; their halls, their chambers, their kitchens, their stanchions, their barns, their cowsheds, their barnyards, their cabbage patches, their plows, their harrows, and the goods and houses that are necessary for their sustenance and welfare.

He was explicit too in the misfortune he intended for the Reivers and their families. In fact on reading this, if there was any power behind the curse it's a wonder the city remains standing:

May all the malevolent wishes and curses ever known, since the beginning of the world, to this hour, light on them. May the malediction of God, that fell upon Lucifer and all his fellows, that cast them from the high Heaven to the deep hell, light upon them.
May the fire and the sword that stopped Adam from the gates of Paradise, stop them from the glory of Heaven, until they forebear, and make amends.

May the evil that fell upon cursed Cain, when he slew his brother Abel, needlessly, fall on them for the needless slaughter that they commit daily.

May the malediction that fell upon all the world, man and beast, and all that ever took life, when all were drowned by the flood of Noah, except Noah and his ark, fall upon them and drown them, man and beast, and make this realm free of them, for their wicked sins.

May the thunder and lightning which rained down upon Sodom and Gomorrah and all the lands surrounding them, and burned them for their vile sins, rain down upon them and burn them for their open sins.

May the evil and confusion that fell on the Gigantis for their oppression and pride in building the Tower of Babylon, confound them and all their works, for their open callous disregard and oppression.

May all the plagues that fell upon Pharaoh and his people of Egypt, their lands, crops and cattle, fall upon them, their equipment, their places, their lands, their crops and livestock.

May the waters of the Tweed and other waters which they use, drown them, as the Red Sea drowned King Pharaoh and the people of Egypt, preserving God's people of Israel.

May the earth open, split and cleave, and swallow them straight to hell, as it swallowed cursed Dathan and Abiron, who disobeyed Moses and the command of God.

May the wild fire that reduced Thore and his followers to two-hundred-fifty in number, and others from 14,000 to 7,000 at anys, usurping against Moses and Aaron, servants of God, suddenly burn and consume them daily, for opposing the commands of God and Holy Church.

May the malediction that suddenly fell upon fair Absalom, riding through the wood against his father, King David, when the branches of a tree knocked him from his horse and hanged him by the hair, fall upon these untrue Scotsmen and hang them the same way, that all the world may see.

May the malediction that fell upon Nebuchadnezzar's lieutenant, Holofernes, making war and savagery upon true Christian men; the malediction that fell upon Judas, Pilate, Herod, and the Jews that crucified Our Lord; and all the plagues and troubles that fell on the city of Jerusalem therefore, and upon Simon Magus for his treachery, bloody Nero, Ditius Magcensius, Olibrius, Julianus Apostita and the rest of the cruel tyrants who slew and murdered Christ's holy servants, fall upon them for their cruel tyranny and murder of Christian people.

And may all the vengeance that ever was taken since the world began, for open sins, and all the plagues and pestilence that ever fell on man or beast, fall on them for their openly evil ways, senseless slaughter and shedding of innocent blood.

I sever and part them from the church of God, and deliver them immediately to the devil of hell, as the Apostle Paul delivered Corinth.

I bar the entrance of all places they come to, for divine service and ministration of the sacraments of holy church, except the sacrament of infant baptism, only; and I forbid all churchmen to hear their confession or to absolve them of their sins, until they are first humbled by this curse.

I forbid all Christian men or women to have any company with them, eating, drinking, speaking, praying, lying, going, standing, or in any other deed-doing, under the pain of deadly sin.

I discharge all bonds, acts, contracts, oaths, made to them by any persons, out of loyalty, kindness, or personal duty, so long as they sustain this cursing, by which no man will be bound to them, and this will be binding on all men.

I take from them, and cast down all the good deeds that ever they did, or shall do, until they rise from this cursing.

I declare them excluded from all matins, masses, evening prayers, funerals or other prayers, on book or bead; of all pigrimages and alms deeds done, or to be done in holy church or be Christian people, while this curse is in effect.

And, finally, I condemn them perpetually to the deep pit of hell, there to remain with Lucifer and all his fellows, and their bodies to the gallows of Burrow moor, first to be hanged, then ripped and torn by dogs, swine, and other wild beasts, abominable to all the world.

And their candle goes from your sight, as may their souls go from the face of God, and their good reputation from the world, until they forebear their open sins, aforesaid, and rise from this terrible cursing and make satisfaction and penance.

In his parish magazine, Vicar Kevin Davies wrote that he thought the Cursing Stone was a 'lethal weapon' and believed the curse should be broken both 'literally and spiritually for all time.'

Some people, it is believed, are the victims of generational-curses such as the one on the Cursing Stone which has been placed on them through no fault of their own but because of the unlawful actions of their ancestors.

Despite all the debating, the town Fathers did not feel there was enough evidence to destroy the stone which still remains at Tully House museum. Apparently Carlisle City Council has requested that the Archbishop of Glasgow lift the old curse just in case it does have any real power.

Mere words perhaps ... and a lot of them ... but this is a curse that was issued by an authoritative figure and being accepted by those hearing it (even if not the Reivers themselves) which is demonstration of the power of words.

And if the curse is true, with it being placed as it is at the heart of Carlisle, between the Castle and the Cathedral, it could be said that it is in a perfect place to cause misfortune on the townspeople.

Ghosts of Carlisle

(Carlisle, 2012)

Other eerie tales from Carlisle include that of ghostly figures seen around the city including an old woman in grey at the Citadel Restaurant. A home in Raffles reported Poltergeist activity in 2007 when Allison Marshall and her four children were so freaked out by supernatural activity occurring in their home that they moved elsewhere. As well as items flying across the room, the property developed strange cold spots, kept seeing flashing lights and a child sobbing could be heard at night. Investigators from the group Scottish Paranormal are said to have put a name to the ghost. It was a former neighbour called Bill.

Captured on CCTV, a ghostly figure can be seen outside a shop on Durranhill Road in Botcherby, Carlisle. In March, 2010, the spirit appearing as a strange mist, drifts in and out of the shop at least ten times in one hour. The same camera seems to show a light coming on in the shop late at night although there was no-one in the shop who could have switched it on. Although there is no explanation for the entity, some people believe it is a ghost that was disturbed by workmen when renovating a flat opposite – which incidentally has a reputation, locally, of being haunted.

At Carlisle Cathedral a former Dean is said to have watched a Monk walking down the aisle and then disappear through a brick wall. Also during a service at the Cathedral, a young girl kept waving at a man no-one else could see. When she was asked to describe him, it was the same ghostly Monk the Dean had seen.

According to ghost tour guide John Robson, the Crown and Mitre Hotel in Carlisle is haunted by at least three ghosts while spirits have also been seen in the cellars at the Citadel Tavern, St Cuthbert's and the Glasshouse Club and these weren't of the alcoholic kind.

The Ghost of Talkin Tarn

Although now a tranquil area of beauty, the hamlet of Talkin was once a busy community. In fact the area was very different in times gone by. Going back to the fourteenth century for instance, the land was rich in coal and lead which will have provided a living for hundreds of miners and their families. While the woodland that surrounded the village provided employment for charcoal-burning.

Pigs and cows will have grazed on the common. It was a time when people and animals lived in close proximity. Living in the village would have been a shoemaker, carpenter and blacksmith. There was no tarn in the fourteenth century, just a village pond that was fed by a spring. Brampton, the closest town had a market (which still continues) where locals could sell their wares and produce.

One elderly woman who lived in Talkin, known as 'Old Martha' would regularly visit Brampton. She kept herself to herself and known for her tendency to fly into tantrums when crossed, few asked about her business. They did however observe her walking to Brampton regularly early in the mornings. She would be carrying butter or cheese produced from her two cows perhaps to sell at the market. Old Martha had no relatives in the village that anyone knew of. What was known was that she was a widow and her husband had died in agony from some unknown illness. It was rumoured that she was a witch and most people avoided her.

One market day Old Martha did not go into Brampton as was her usual routine. Later in the day some people of the village saw her near her home looking unwell. Her face and neck were swollen and covered in a rash. Over the next few days she was seen visiting the spring, the main water supply for the community. Although her rash and the swelling subsided, it left her with ugly red blotches on her face and neck.

Then the people of the village started to become ill. Their faces and necks became swollen with a red rash appearing that turned black just before they died a terrible death. It became known as the 'plague' or the 'black death' and eventually whole families were almost wiped out by the plague.

Who or what was the cause of this terrible illness? The village began questioning their misfortune and they remembered that the first person who had been seen to have it in the village was Old Matha but she hadn't died.

This seemed to confirm the villagers' suspicion that the old woman was a witch. They wanted her out of their village and poor Martha who had not been included in these discussions and who was just getting on with her daily life without bothering anyone will have had no idea why the whole village had suddenly turned against her.

She was confused, probably frightened and upset by their hostile attitude. When they approached her, she had to stand and try to defend herself against all her neighbours who were angrily throwing accusations at her and as tempers flared, they began throwing stones at her. This caused her to step backward towards the edge of the pond. As more stones flew in her direction she fell into the water. The villagers watched as she vanished into the dark pool.

Then she surfaced and someone heard her calling something like "Clean water: you must use clean water."

They heard her words but did not try to help her. Angry, suspicious and scared they allowed the old woman to drown. Then, putting two plus two together and coming up with five, the villagers decided that this was an explanation as to why old Martha always used the spring and never the pond. She had fouled the pond water and caused the death of so many members of their families. This was their justification as to why they had stood and watched her drown without coming to her aid. She was evil and she had deserved to die.

They returned home and that night it rained as it had never rained before. The village became waterlogged. The one spring that supplied the pond became two. Over the days that followed, two springs became three and three became four. The level of the pond began to rise and within days the entire village was submerged. The villagers saved what they could from their homes but because of the flood within days they had lost their homes and their livelihoods.

The water never subsided. The village pond had become a tarn and has remained that way ever since. Villagers were offered temporary homes in nearby Brampton and some found shelter where they could. Some began rebuilding on higher ground, the foundation of the present day Talkin Village.

Rumours tell of people, who visiting Talkin Tarn on the anniversary of Old Martha's drowning have heard her words 'clean water, more water' repeated over and over and thus the urban legend was born that there is a whole village sitting at the bottom of Talkin Tarn. A crashed helicopter is also said to lie at the bottom of the lake.

The Brampton Witch

(Vintage postcard: Brampton 1940s copyright unknown)

Brampton, the market town near Talkin village is not without its ghosts, perhaps the most famous being Lizzie Baty, also known as the Brampton Witch or the Wise Woman of Brampton. Her story is linked with a cursed tea set that it is said to bring its owners whomever they may be, doom and disaster.

Lizzie Baty, according to legend, was married to the headmaster of Brampton School, John Baty. She was a well-known figure in the town and some thought she had magic powers. When a market stallholder stopped giving Lizzie her rations of butter, the stallholder suddenly found that she couldn't get her lard to set. A young bride-to-be from Brampton was told by Lizzie that she would get a 'white dress soon enough' but the dress was not her wedding dress. It turned out to be a funeral gown.

Lizzie Baty, they said, could look into the future. Lizzy Baty, they said, would curse anyone who crossed her.

In 1817, 88 year old Lizzie Baty asked for her friend John Parker to come to her cottage at Craw Hall. Lying on her death bed, she gave a faint smile when her builder friend entered her room and asked him to come closer. She wanted John to have her tea set but he needed to remember that this wasn't any ordinary tea set. It was bound by a curse. Lizzie told him that drinking from the fine china cups would bring good luck to any member of his family. However, if the tea set ever left the family, it would bring doom and disaster to the new owner.

The Parker family took this warning seriously and almost 200 years later the tea set with its large square teapot and delicate pattern around the top edge which is carried through to the milk jug, sugar bowl, cups and saucers is still in pristine condition and being looked after by subsequent generations.

Jim Parker Templeton's mother was John Parker's great niece. His sister Marion inherited the antique tea set and on her death, left it to another member of their family.

Jim feels he owes his life to the tea set. When war was declared in 1939, Jim was one of the first groups of young men to be called up to fight. Before going off to war, his mother Mary wanted to feel he had luck on his side. She told Jim to cycle from their house in Belle Vue, Carlisle to a relative's home in Brampton and to ask for a cup of tea from the china. At the time Jim wasn't convinced the china could bring him luck but by the time he had cycled the ten miles to Brampton he was ready for a drink and enjoyed a welcome cup of tea from the china tea set.

(Table set for tea as in 1900s)

Not long after, Jim joined the Royal Medical Corps and was one of only 37 men out of 500 who returned to England at the end of the war in 1945. Jim explained they lost a lot of men in the battle of Salerno in southern Italy. He also described getting 'feelings' while on duty, as if something was prompting him to move and as he did, a shell would land in the place he'd been standing. This he said happened a few times.

On returning home he wondered if the china tea set maybe had brought him luck. He married and had three daughters but understandably, none of his family was keen to take on the china which, as well as bringing luck, could bring disaster if it falls into the wrong hands. Even so it is said to remain within the Parker family.

The Croglin Vampire

The Croglin Vampire was first spoken of in Augustus Hare's book called 'In My Solitary Life.' Augustus, born in 1834 was a writer and raconteur. His written work includes accounts of his visits to eerie places such as Chillingham Castle, the Otterburn moors, Gibside, Dunstanburgh and Holy Island. Augustus, according to his book, was told the story of the Croglin Beast by Captain Fisher whose family owned the one-storey house, Croglin Grange.

The tale which is likely to have provided excellent post-dinner entertainment for the men while smoking their cigars and drinking brandy may have been told a number of times.

Seemingly during its long existence and despite the large grounds it stood in, Croglin Grange had always just had one floor. Its terrace looked out over the grounds that swept down towards the Church in the hollow. A wooded area separated their lawn from the churchyard.

There are a number of versions of this story and some say that village rumours spoke of something strange and dangerous making periodic attacks on people and animals in the area even before the incident within this eerie tale.

When the Fisher family outgrew Croglin Grange, instead of adding another floor as some wealthy families would be inclined to do, they moved elsewhere and let Croglin Grange to two brothers Mike and Edward Cranswell and their sister Amelia. The tenants gained a good reputation within the community. They were kind and generous and they seemed to be delighted with their new home.

During their first winter at Croglin, they joined in with village activities and were often seen at social gatherings. The following summer was glorious and one hot day the brothers lay under the trees with their books while Amelia sat doing her needlework. It was too hot for any kind of physical activity. They dined early then went back to sit outside before retiring for the night.

Amelia found it so hot she couldn't sleep. She had closed her windows but not the shutters. Looking out of the window at the summer night she became aware of two lights flickering in and out of the trees at the bottom of their lawn, beyond which was the churchyard. She watched as a dark shadow emerged from the trees and looked as if it was making its way towards the house. Feeling uneasy she bolted her bedroom door and went to bed.

She began to drift off to sleep when she was jolted awake by a strange scratching sound at her window. Looking in that direction, she saw a hideous looking face with flaming red eyes glaring at her. Amelia was frozen with fear as she was gripped by an uncontrollable horror. She wanted to scream but nothing came out.

Then the scratching sound gave way to a pick-pick-picking sound and the terrified girl realised the creature was unpicking the lead of the window until a glass pane fell onto the carpet in the room and a long bony finger reached inside to turn the handle of the window. It opened and the creature came in.

Paralysed with fear she watched as the towering figure of a man whose skin was pale and almost translucent and whose burning eyes never left her made his way towards the bed. As he reached her, the creature wound her hair around his bony fingers, pulled her head to one side and bent towards her throat as if to deliver a kiss. As he bit her violently in the throat, Amelia found her voice again and she screamed and screamed until her brothers came to her room. The door was still locked but they broke it open. By then the creature had made its escape through the window and their sister, bleeding profusely from the wound in her throat, was lying unconscious.

One brother ran after the creature which fled into the night and disappeared over the wall into the churchyard. He returned to his sister's room. It was a bad wound but she was a strong woman and eventually when she came round she insisted she was shaken but they shouldn't worry about her. She felt too that there would be an explanation for her ghastly experience. It had probably been an escaped lunatic from some asylum in the area.

Amelia's wound slowly healed and she seemed to get better but her doctor felt the shock will have affected her more than she admitted and suggested she needed a change of environment to recover mentally and physically. Her brothers took her to Switzerland.

They all enjoyed their spell in Switzerland and while there the boys purchased two Swiss pistols and ammunition. In the autumn they returned to Croglin Grange. They had liked it there and after all, lunatics did not escape every day! Even so they were prepared, should such an incident occur again. When the family returned to Croglin Grange, the boys occupying a room opposite their sister's and always they kept loaded pistols in their room.

The winter passed without incident but in the spring, Amelia was woken up by a scratch, scratching sound at her window and saw the same hideous face and red eyes glaring at her. This time she screamed loudly, alerting her brothers who ran out of the house with their pistols. As the creature fled, one bullet hit the hideous being in the leg but it still managed to pull itself over the wall into the churchyard.

Another version of the story suggests that the brothers had sworn revenge on the creature who had hurt their sister. So this time, when he visited, the two boys had been lying in wait in the shadows and as the creature stepped into the room they both used their pistols against it. After giving out a low howl, the creature fled in the direction of the churchyard.

The next day, the brothers, joined by other villagers went to the churchyard and searched around for signs of the creature. After searching the churchyard they went inside the silent church. Someone noticed the crypt door was slightly ajar and making their way inside they were met with a horrific scene. It was full of coffins that had been opened, their horribly mangled and distorted contents scattered all over the floor. Only one coffin standing alone was intact. The lid had been lifted but still lay loosely over the coffin.

Someone raised the lid. And there lying shrivelled, withered and mummified was the same hideous creature that had broken into Croglin Grange. In its leg could be seen marks of a recent pistol shot. The crowd, recognising the creature as being a vampire dragged the coffin and its demonic contents outside and burned the lot to ashes.

In another version of the story, the villagers carried the demon creature to the nearest crossroads, dismembered it, beheaded it and staked it through the heart before burning the remains.

There is no explanation of where the strange creature came from although Patricia and Lionel Fanthorpe carried out research that verifies that a Hare lady (same surname as Augustus Hare who had written about this story) had married a Captain Fisher who'd once lived in Croglin Grange.

Although Croglin Grange is now a two-storeyed house, it seems the second floor had been added some time long ago during the building's ancient history. Although there is no church nearby, there are the remains of an old church in some land not far away from the house. Apparently this church had ceased to be used after Cromwell's men had damaged it following the Civil War in the 17th Century.

Their conclusion was that although Hare's story suggests the vampire incident took place towards the end of the 19th century it is more likely to have happened in the 17th. It is possible that Captain Fisher was relating a story which had been passed down through his family and therefore taking the actual incident a few centuries rather than a few years, back.

Haunted Hospitals and Care Homes

Many staff working in hospitals and care homes seem to accept hauntings as a natural part of their working experience. When talking to these people I get the impression they have experienced so many 'unexplained' happenings within their workplace that they don't even question it any more. They just accept it to the point where they might come out with, for instance, "Hannah's up to her old tricks, again" when referring to the late Hannah who continued her habit of leaving taps on when she was alive, even after she had departed.

My daughter described many such tales to me from the times when she worked in care homes in the North of England, including this one about Ethel who just didn't know when to say goodbye …

Shortly after starting at a new care home, my daughter was told by her colleagues that often, when a resident passes away, their soul is unable to leave this world until their bedroom window is opened and they are told firmly to go. At the time, my daughter didn't believe in ghosts and reacted with scepticism thinking her workmates were teasing her. Then when she witnessed her colleagues actually carrying out this ritual whenever there was a death in the care home, she thought they'd just gone slightly mad – too many long night shifts had got to them!

However, one night at the start of my daughter's shift, she was given the sad news that one of their residents had died. This particularly lady had been in room number five so when the nurse-call buzzer for that room sounded, she thought it rather unusual.

Nonetheless, she and a colleague went to investigate. Once in the room they were greeted with nothing except an eerie chill. There were no staff around and no wandering residents who may have set off the alarm; nothing. Puzzled, they reset the buzzer and left the room. They didn't get very far down the corridor before the alarm sounded once more.

They went back to the room and again, all was silent. The room was empty. This happened eight times in total before my daughter decided to take drastic action! Striding back into the room after responding to the buzzer one more time and feeling rather stupid, she flung the window wide open. "Right then Dora," she shouted. "You have to go now. We have to say goodbye. It's time for you to find your new home."

Amazingly, after giving her little speech after opening the window, the alarm never sounded again that night.

An older care assistant, Heather, used to do agency care assistant work when she was in her 20s. She occasionally worked in a War Memorial hospital. One night she was on a ward for the first time. When things were quiet the staff would occasionally take the chance to get some sleep. The new night staff would use the on-call room to rest in whereas this room (Heather noticed later) was never used by nurses who had been there for some time. They would either sleep in the small office or not at all.

Heather was on a break so she thought she'd get her head down and went to the on-call room. As she was drifting off to sleep she heard the door open and someone walk in. She thought it was one of the nurses looking for her to do a job and decided to keep her eyes closed to pretend to be asleep so they wouldn't disturb her. Although she had her eyes closed she could still feel a presence in the room and could hear a person walking around. They started fiddling with the blinds on the window and this started to annoy Heather. She pulled the light blanket she had covered herself with over her face and mumbled "I'm trying to sleep. Do you mind?" The annoying sound stopped, she heard the door open and then there was silence. She gathered that whomever had entered had left again. She drifted off to sleep.

When she returned to the ward she asked the staff whether they knew who had come into the room, wondering what they had wanted. No-one admitted to it. She wondered if it could have been a patient but was told that this wouldn't be possible as the room was behind the nurse's station and wasn't accessible to anyone else. Besides there had always been someone in the nurse's station while she'd been asleep. No-one had seen anyone enter the room or for that matter open the door.

During the course of the night the other staff started taking their breaks and one of the new nurses went to the on-call room to get some sleep. After around 45 minutes there was a scream from the room. The nurse had woken up to see a heavily-built man standing looking out of the window which was beside the bed. When she reached out to touch him, he vanished.

Apparently, when talking about the incident, the nurses who'd been there for some time all know this happened occasionally but they didn't expect anyone would believe them. So rather than telling the new girls of what they might experience when using the on-call room, they preferred that they discovered it for themselves!

Haunted Hospitals

Many of the old hospitals and institutions in the UK have been closed down, restored or demolished, depending on the likely costs of renovation and upkeep of these ancient buildings and subject to their listed building status. It is no surprise that paranormal activity is reported around these areas where not only have people moved on to the other side but where a touch of darkness and despair pervades.

In some asylums, post-war single mothers were forced to give up their babies for adoption. In the early 1900s, mental hospitals became the testing grounds for controversial treatments such as lobotomies and electroconvulsive therapy. Women would be labelled insane and locked up in asylums for having postnatal depression and even for social transgressions such as infidelity. In fact anyone who could persuade two doctors to sign a certificate of insanity could have a loved one or relative put away in a mental institution.

These are places where walls echoed with horror, loneliness, fear and social isolation and where patients weren't always treated with respect and dignity. At night, hospitals can be spooky places and many that are still standing in the UK have their ghost stories.

A Veteran ghost hunter, the late Andrew Green, felt that because of the pain, unhappiness and distress associated with hospitals, paranormal activity within their walls is due to a form of electromagnetic energy: an echo of the intensely stressful experiences people went through during the time they were in the hospital. He collected many stories relating to hospitals and institutions in the UK, some that can be explained, some that stubbornly defy any rational explanation.

Although many doctors and nursing staff will dismiss ghost stories relating to hospitals as nonsense there are others who would dispute this. Judith Whalley, risk manager at the City Hospital in Birmingham told reporters of a ghostly encounter in a top floor corridor of the hospital. As she was walking, she noticed a ward sister coming from the opposite direction towards her. Ms Whalley nodded and said "Evening sister," as they passed each other. At the same time, she realised she could only see the nurse from the knees up. It is possible that because the building was very old and new floors had been added over the years, the ghost may have been walking along an older floor level.

Ms whalley also reports that a group of builders once disturbed something while demolishing wards that had originally been a part of the workhouse. The men heard cries coming from inside one of the wards and when they went to investigate, the building was empty. No-one was there and yet when they returned to the door to leave, they found it was locked. A sense of panic quivered around the group as they knew that demolition was imminent. They could hear the demolition ball heading their way. They managed to break the door down and escape but insisted that a priest be called in to carry out an exorcism or they would not work there again.

Still in Birmingham and during the building of the Birmingham Eye Centre in 1996, alarm bells were triggered at the site (which was being monitored by CCTV) when a ghostly grey figure was spotted. Security guards who went to investigate found no-one was there.

The now demolished Hackney Hospital in London, originally built in 1930 as a workhouse and later used as a hospital, was described as a 'hellhole' by former staff who worked there. Green's reports include those from nurses on night-shift who felt someone tap them on their shoulders but when they turned around, no-one was there. Staff also had their suspicions as to who this ghost could be. Apparently, a nurse on night-shift was bottle-feeling a baby in the Maternity Wing. She dozed off and slumped forward in her sleep, smothering the baby. Horrified by what she had done she committed suicide but continued to walk the wards, tapping sleepy nurses on their shoulders to keep them from falling asleep on duty.

A strong smell of violet perfume usually comes just before the appearance of a ghostly nurse at Scunthorpe General who seems to have healing powers. This ghost often appears when a baby is desperately ill and after her visit, the baby usually recovers.

In 2009 the Times reported tales of spooky happenings at the Derby Royal Hospital. Managers began to receive complaints from nervous workers about a figure wearing a black cloak that was stalking the wards and walking through walls. Although the hospital denied that there would be an official exorcism, a spokesperson for the Bishop of Derby confirmed that the hospital's on-site chaplain had requested advice from the diocese Paranormal Advisor.

Cane Hill Asylum, Surrey

Several decades ago, before it shut down, a relative of the writer, Susan, trained as a psychiatric nurse at Cane Hill Hospital, Coulsdon Surrey. Opened in 1882 the Asylum could hold up to 2000 patients in its 40 wards and stood within 43 acres of land. Some of its patients were the relatives of celebrities including Charlie Chaplin's mother Hannah, David Bowie's half-brother and Michael Caine's half-brother.

Cane Hill had a reputation for being one of the most atmospheric Victorian asylums in England. In the 1960s the land was farmed, it had a dairy and the hospital was almost self-sufficient for food and milk. Cliff Meredith began his electrician's apprenticeship in the late 1970s and got a job at Cane Hill. He remembers being called in to fix a light that had blown in the mortuary. He wouldn't go alone and even with company he found the place eerie. Over the years, as the place was being emptied it had a distinctly strange feel about it. Staff reported hearing sounds, doors would slam shut although there was no-one there and people felt they were being watched. The hospital gained a reputation for being haunted.

The building was falling to pieces and could not continue as a hospital without having a lot of money spent on it. Susan lived in Cane Hill while she trained and she remembers how cold and stark her room was and how the floors filled with cockroaches at night.

After the hospital was shut down, reports of ghostly sightings continued even while the building lay derelict. One of the security team for instance was patrolling the grounds with the guard dog one dark night. The dog was let off its leash and immediately began running away in the opposite direction whimpering. The security guard looked in the direction the dog was scarpering from and noticed the figure of a man wandering around the trees. When he went to the spot where the man had been seen, he found a grave of the hospital's first superintendent, Sir James Moody. The grave was almost hidden in the undergrowth.

Keith Boutcher, while making a film intended as a permanent visual record of Cane Hill before the building was demolished, was at the hospital site with his wife when she saw a figure cross the corridor ahead of them. When the couple when to check who this might be, there was no-one there.

Although demolished in 2008 photographs and videos have been published on the internet showing how the building had been simply deserted, a lot of the hospital equipment, beds, filing cabinets and patient's possessions having been left as they stood. Many felt it was a shame such a grand Victorian building was pulled down and considered unworthy of renovation. Several orbs can be seen on photographs taken in the mortuary while a misty spectre and ghostly images were captured in the Chapel and other rooms of the derelict building.

Angelic Paranormal Activity

A report commissioned in 2010 by the TV Show Supernatural into 'angelic paranormal activity in the UK' noted that there had been 755 documented incidents in the past 25 years ranging from visions of angels and animal spirits to helpful and healing entities.

Extensive research conducted by Lionel Fanthorpe included studying archives, police reports, published reports and interviews with ex-police officers. From this Fanthorpe observed a series of 'hotspots' where guardian angels and fairies seem to congregate in the UK.

One of the positive hotspots is St Martin's Church in Westmeston in Sussex. Here there has been dozens of reports of a friendly phantom drifting across the churchyard. Another friendly ghost that glides around a graveyard apparently smiling at people who have recently been bereaved was witnessed at St Botolph's Priory in Colchester, Essex.

According to this report, not all ghostly sightings are evil, terrifying or threatening. Many ghostly sightings reported involved a harmless spirit such as the phantom seen gliding from St Martin's Churchyard in Sussex. This eerie spectre then drifts across the road before vanishing through the wall of a neighbouring house. These Benign Spirits were the most common reported incidents with 192 reports.

The next most reported angelic paranormal experience is that of the Friendly Entity of which 127 reports were received in the last 25 years. Among the Friendly Entities the report describes that of a helpful butler who answers the door of the Manor House in Cold Ashton where motorists regularly knock to ask for help with directions. He always points them in the right direction even though no-one lives at the Manor House which has been derelict for years.

There were 104 reports of Angel Visions. Then, the next most reported supernatural occurrence is that of Helpful Entities in which ghostly phantoms help save the lives of people who come into contact with them. 99 reports received. Also included were 69 cases of animal spirits, 44 sightings of fairies, 41 visions of saints, 32 encounters with white witches, 24 visitations by guardian angels and 23 healing entities.

Several walkers have reported seeing a Monk spirit wearing a large gold cross in Sutton Wood. The Monk features among the angelic visions as those who see him describe the vision as being very holy with an aura of goodness that makes them glad they have seen it.

A fairy is regularly seen in the woods in Croston, Lancashire according to 44 official reports. Known to the locals as Shrewfoot, this is said to be a very protective entity and is documented to have saved at least one pedestrian who was in danger on an adjacent road, from a speeding lorry.

Among the 69 animal spirits reported is that of Greyfriar's Bobby in Edinburgh Scotland, a skye Terrier who belonged to a man called John Gray. (See part II of this book). When John died in 1858 his dog guarded his grave for fourteen years until his death in 1872. Reports describe witnesses having seen the phantom of John's faithful terrier still loyally guarding his last resting place in Greyfriars Cemetery, Edinburgh.

Big Cat Sightings ... Are they Ghosts or are they real?

Five or six years ago in Roadhead, Cumbria John was driving along the road and a huge cat ran across the road in front of the car. He watched as it pushed through hedgerow and vanished into the field beyond. Not only was he amazed by the size of it but there was something unnerving about the experience, as if it was supernatural.

It's an experience he has never forgotten and this led him to do a little research to find out whether anyone else had seen anything similar. What he found was there had been many big cat sightings in Cumbria previous to his own experience and since. These curious alien creatures have been spotted in Bewcastle, Witherslack, Kendal, Levans, Natland and in the Winster Valley. Maureen, a resident of Penrith tells of how one evening she saw a strange black cat-like creature in a field. Although it was some distance away she feels it was too large to be an ordinary cat and mentioned that it had a slinky, panther-like motion. It was like no creature she had seen before in the fields and she was too frightened to move any closer towards it.

Another witness describes how he was travelling home one evening when a fox ran out front of his car. He braked to avoid hitting the animal. At that same moment a large black puma-like creature suddenly appeared from the side of the road chasing after the fox.

In 2009 a number of people saw a large puma-like creature on the waste ground near the Cumberland Infirmary at Carlisle, Cumbria. It was described as being black, definitely feline but as large as a Labrador dog. Police tried to track the strange creature but were unable to find anything.

Then one night at dusk in April, 2010 Jeni Banks was driving home to Wetheral in Cumbria, when she noticed a large dark creature in the road ahead. Her description is very much like accounts of similar experiences by other witnesses: the cat was black, around the size of a Labrador. Its eyes gleamed in her car's headlights and Jeni was astounded by its long black body and its powerful, curling tail. She saw it clearly before it vanished into the woodland. She described the experience as surreal.

In recent years it seems like more and more big cat sightings are being reported. In 2012 in Whitehaven, for instance, while driving from Arlecdon to Whitehaven, just as he had driven over the bridge at the bottom of the hill, someone spotted a cat the size of a huge dog coming out of the hedge and onto the road. The cat was described as being light brown with a long thick tail.

And while jogging on Scot Scar late in the day in 2012, Angela Jones and Eve Grayson were terrified when a huge mysterious black cat crossed their path. The girls described it as being about the size of a Labrador dog, jet black with long legs. When they switched on their torch, two orange eyes stared back at them. Since it was standing in their way, they cautiously moved towards it when its tail started to sway threateningly and its fur bristled similar to how a cat behaves when it is hostile. Real or ghostly, the girls felt panicked by the unearthly beast's aggression and turned around and ran.

It was dark which will have added to the eeriness of the experience but both girls were unnerved by what they had encountered and felt inspired to search on the internet to find out whether there had been any previous big cat sightings, to find like John in Roadhead, that there were many local reports.

February 2012 is when a bus driver, Steve Allison, saw a large black panther-like creature in a field not far from Carlisle. He was about half a mile away from the small village of Rockcliff when he noticed the creature ahead of him in the field. Although it was lying he could tell it wasn't small. The sound of the bus approaching must have startled it as it got up and sprinted away. It had a shiny black coat and a curly tail. And like others who had been through similar experiences, he admitted that the beast was so scary he wouldn't even have considered getting off the bus to get close to it.

In August, 2012 while driving on the new Carlisle Bypass, not far from Asda, Raymond Sant and his wife Vera reported seeing a large black cat, the size of a Labrador cross the road. It had a long tail and looked very much like a panther.

As with all bizarre sightings, explanations are sought and some think that it could be possible that big cats are in fact breeding and living in the wild. Others ask: do they really exist? After all the only evidence collected so far is eye-witness testimonies and not even a paw-print. Like the Beast of Bodmin Moor – which after a government investigation was declared a myth – could these big cat sightings be real, supernatural or a myth?

Granddad is Never Far Away

When Paul married Emma he hadn't quite bargained for the ghosts that are never far away from her. At first he lightly dismissed it when she would tell him that her granddad had visited although he had died when she'd been a young girl. Paul didn't believe in ghosts and preferred not to encourage Emma's apparent easy acceptance that their house in Cumbria was haunted.

Things would often go missing around the house but Paul was always sure there'd be a logical explanation. One day he lost his mobile phone although he knew exactly where he'd left it. Only it wasn't there. They searched everywhere; turned the house upside down looking for it and eventually after three weeks decided to buy a new one. The next day, Paul noticed the missing mobile on the top of a cabinet in their bedroom. It had not been there previously and just seemed to have appeared out of nowhere.

Objects got moved about the house, pictures were moved slightly while they were out and electronic gadgets would break down for no apparent reason. But still Paul didn't believe in ghosts.

Emma's father didn't believe in ghosts either. He laughed when his wife mentioned that not only was Emma's house haunted but they knew the ghost was her granddad, his father. "Impossible," he responded. "She's just making it up. There's no such thing as ghosts."

But his wife knew differently. Because when Emma was young, she used to describe how her granddad would come into her bedroom at night and sit on the bed beside her. Or he would stand and watch over her, smiling. The young girl was never spooked by the experience. She accepted it as a normal occurrence and because she would tell her mother this in such a matter-of-fact way, her mother never discouraged her from sharing. She actually believed Emma was telling the truth.

So when at the age of 20 Emma and her mother were in the kitchen washing dishes one day and Emma mentioned totally out of the blue, "Granddad came to see me last night," her mother just smiled. She knew what she was talking about without having to ask. When Emma asked if she remembered how he would come to her when she was young her mother nodded. Of course she did. What did surprise her mother was that granddad had visited her in a different house. But he hadn't had any problem finding his granddaughter. Emma described how she'd been lying awake in bed when she watched him come through the door and walk to her side.

After the birth of their first child, Emma noticed how he would often chat away to a specific corner of the living room or towards the rocking chair in his bedroom as if talking to someone. Paul began to notice it too. They would listen to the baby monitor and it was apparent to both that he would be talking to someone, listening and answering questions. He would say it was "granddad" when asked and he recognised photographs of Emma's granddad as the man who visited him in his room.

Emma's friends started to accept her house was haunted. How couldn't they when they'd be sitting and a framed photograph would suddenly fly across the room and land on the floor? There'd be no-one near the place where it had been sitting. Some would hear footsteps on the stairs but the most obvious sound of his presence would be the sound of coins falling and jingling on the wood floor of the passageway. No matter how thorough they searched, there would be nothing there. Paul began to accept their home was haunted.

One day, while discussing the ghost, Emma's mother described to her husband the sound like coins on the wood flooring whenever her granddad 'visited.' That's when he suddenly acknowledged, "Yes, it is my dad?" His amazed wife asked "How is that?" and he explained:

"Whenever my dad visited anyone and they weren't in, he would put a penny on the door handle. So when they came home and opened the door, the penny would drop to let them know he had visited."

The hauntings continued but no one was ever spooked by this friendly visitor. People would talk to him, greet him and accept his presence when they felt him in the room. Objects stopped going missing and there were no frustrating disturbances, perhaps because he had made his point: granddad was near and nearby he would always stay.

Because when they moved house, Granddad happily moved with them. Emma would get little 'messages' that she could interpret to know he was near. But not only is their new home haunted by her granddad but another elderly man, Clive, has just moved in. This is the ghost of the old man who lived in the house prior to them. A medium picked up on him but Emma already knew he was there. He had loved his home and she doesn't mind sharing it with her ghostly friends as long as they don't make a nuisance of themselves.

Like the time when they were only just starting to be aware of Clive. Emma was having coffee with a friend in the living room. Their children were playing in the passageway and both women heard the children refer to Clive by name as if talking to him. When the women went into the passage, the door of the electric cupboard which contained all the circuit boxes was standing open. The women were surprised because the door is really stiff and difficult to open and had been firmly closed earlier. Often Emma can't manage to open it on her own. They asked the children who had opened the door and both replied in chorus: "Clive!"

This is when Emma had to tell Clive that he was very welcome in their home but would he please not do anything to put their safety at risk. After this, the family settled very happily into their new home and if occasionally they are visited by their friendly ghosts, even Paul, who is now a member of a paranormal investigative team and slowly developing his own mediumistic gift, is happy to accept it.

The Ghost Village of Imber

(Imber photographs donated to Wiltshire Heritage Museum by Rex Sawyer and Rosalind Hooper)

Up until the Second World War, there was a permanent small community in Imber since 967AD. During the Second World War the village was seized by the government so the vast area of empty land that surrounded the village could be used to train American troops. People who lived in the village were given four weeks to leave. Villagers thought that one day they would be allowed to return but because of the danger of unexploded bombs, there is restricted access to the area. With regular reports of paranormal activity in the area, Imber has truly become a ghost village.

Most of the former residents have now died and yet people have reported hearing the sounds of chatter and laughter coming from the empty buildings at night, especially where the old pub once stood. Ghosts believed to haunt the deserted village are Major Whistler who was once the wealthiest person living there. He owned the town hall and the Imber Court Building. Some mornings people visit the village to find graffiti has appeared on the sides of the buildings overnight and the court is one the buildings that is often covered with graffiti. Because the graffiti usually describes the purposes of the buildings, it is thought that the ghosts of former residents are haunting the village where they once lived, Major Whistler being one of them.

Another former resident Albert Nash was the village blacksmith. People liked and respected Albert who would fix equipment and machinery from nearby farms. When the village was forced to evacuate, he almost instantly suffered from a mental breakdown. The blacksmith became very ill and six weeks after moving out of his home, he died. The official cause of death was of a 'broken heart'. At night, the metallic clanging that can be heard is attributed to Albert and his ghost is often blamed for supernatural events occurring near where his workshop used to be.

On handing the village back over to one of the Range Wardens, after an army exercise a soldier was standing outside Imber Court, waiting for the Range Warden to check inside for cleanliness. Imber Court had been originally the medieval Lord's manor in Saxon times and was rebuilt during the 18th century. The man refused to go in on his own. When asked why the Range Warden admitted that a few years ago he was upstairs closing a shutter that had been left open. A voice from behind him asked in his ear "What gives you the right?" The voice was as clear as day but on turning around no-one was there. No-one was heard to walk away and the Warden knew he was the only person in the building.

A paranormal investigator decided to make use of one of the few days Imber is open to the public to discover whether the village is really haunted. His intention was to spend the night at the village pub which, standing next to the graveyard is reputed to be haunted. He checked the building to make certain there was no-one else around and also checked the door to see if it was locked. There were eerie sounds, some like a human groaning but he was able to establish that these came from a metal door banging in the wind. Throughout the night he was able to find a reason for most noises he heard. In the early hours of the morning the wind died down and there was an eerie silence about the place. He decided to call it a day and drove away. As he turned back to look at the village he felt as if he was being watched and that there was something very strange about the place even though he never saw any ghostly presences that night.

The village remains deserted. The UK Ministry of Defence has built new houses at Imber that are windowless and empty to create a replica village for mock battles and target practice. Villagers were never allowed to return but the graveyard is apparently still in use.

Haunted Chagford

(Chagford – Vintage Postcard)

The village of Chagford on the edge of Dartmoor which is steeped in legend, history and ghostly goings-on has been named one of the most haunted villages in England. Although often referred to as a village, Chagford was actually made a town in 1305 when a Charter from king Edward I decreed it should be one of four Dartmoor towns licensed for the 'stamping' of tin and the collection of the royal tin tax.

Why is Chagford so rich in hauntings? Colin Wilson as Vice-President of the Ghost Club Society noted that when scientists researched into haunted sites, they found strong magnetic fields. After extensive research Wilson concluded that Chagford is a strongly haunted place and he puts this down to the magnetism in the granite which surrounds the area. Dowsers call them ley lines and apparently the whole area around Chagford is surrounded by them. Ley lines seem to provide the ideal environment for ghosts and paranormal activity. Chagford, according to Wilson is a place full of recordings: echoes of the past.

One of the most famous ghosts of Chagford is that of a Cavalier who haunts the Three Crowns Hotel; a building that has been standing since the 13th century. This ghost is believed to be the poet Sidney Godolphin who fought as a Cavalier in the English Civil War. Godolphin was mortally wounded in February, 1643 during a battle in Chagford that took place around the large stone porch of the building that is now the Three Crowns.

This gentle and sensitive man who probably stood little chance in the harsh world of warfare, died of his wound on the cold granite floor of the porch. His ghost often returns to the scene of his death and as well as haunting the porch, his regal figure dressed in flamboyant cavalier uniform has been seen by staff and guests in rooms of the hotel. Landlord and owner of the hotel John Giles insists he does not believe in ghosts and yet he has seen the Cavalier. When they first moved into the hotel some decades ago, he was going down the corridor from his bedroom when he saw the Cavalier silhouetted in white. The experience put the hairs up on the back of his neck and when he returned to his bedroom he was all 'goosy-pimpled.'

Another Chagford ghost is that of Mary Whiddon whose violent death is believed to be the inspiration behind a part of the plot in RD Blackmore's novel *Lorna Doone*. One sunny day in 1641, a happy young girl made her way to St Michael's Church in anticipation of her wedding ceremony. On reaching the church, she walked up the aisle to the altar where her handsome groom stood waiting for her. After the wedding ceremony the couple left the church, walking out into the bright Dartmoor sunshine, Mary perhaps admiring the gleaming ring now on the third finger of her left hand. But no sooner had she looked up to smile at her new husband than a bullet hit her and she crumpled to the ground. A jealous lover had taken aim at the bridegroom but missed and hit Mary instead. The young woman was carried across the road to the Three Crowns Hotel where she was pronounced dead.

According to legend, any girl who is married at the Three Crowns Hotel will meet the ghost of Mary Whiddon. Her ghost is also said to haunt the Bishop's Room and the upstairs corridors of the hotel.

A memorial at the church for Mary Whiddon reads:

Here lieth Mary the daughter of Oliver Whyddon Esquire who died the 11th day of October Anodm 1641. Reader wouldst know who here is laid Behold a Matron yet a maid A modest look a pious heart A Mary for the better part But drie thine eyes why wilt thou weep Such damsels doe not die but sleepe

Radiant boys

During a conversation in a local group, the ghost of Corby Castle, near Wetheral in Cumbria was mentioned. This led me to delve deeper into a branch of ghosts in England called "Radiant Boys." These are purportedly the spirits of boys who were murdered by their own mothers. The counties of Cumbria and Northumberland appear to have more than the usual share of these kind of hauntings, Corby Castle being the most well known for being haunted by a Radiant Boy.

Corby Castle was originally a 14th century tower house which in the 19th century was transformed into a splendid country mansion. Many years ago a clergyman, the Reverend Henry Redburgh, Rector of Greystoke, and his wife were staying at Corby Castle when during their first night, the holy man was woken up in the early hours of the morning to see a glowing boy, all in white with golden hair, standing watching over him.

He reported that soon after falling asleep, probably between one and two in the morning, he awoke to notice the fire was totally extinguished and therefore gave out no light. Yet he could see a glimmer in the centre of the room which increased to a bright flame. He was worried something had caught fire so took a closer look and to his amazement saw a beautiful boy, clothed in white, with bright locks of golden hair standing by his bedside. The boy stood there for some time staring at the reverend with a mild yet benevolent expression. He then glided towards the chimney and disappeared.

The Reverend found the room was once again in total darkness and swears this to be a true account of his experience upon his word as a clergyman. Without explanation, the

Reverend and his wife left in a hurry the next morning and it was some time later that the family learned the true reason for his departure. The Radiant Boy has also been seen by several members of the Howard family who owned the building up until 1994.

The haunted room forms part of the old house having windows looking out over the courtyard. The room is next to a tower which has walls that are approximately eight to ten feet thick and a winding staircase. It is accessible from a passage cut through the thick wall.

This room, which was once furnished with an old-fashioned bed and dark furniture is said to have had an air of gloom which may have given rise to several unaccountable reports of apparitions and noises that guests staying at Corby Castle reported to the owners. The Clergyman is therefore not the only guest to have witnessed paranormal activity in Corby Castle. Friends of the Reverend confirmed that his conviction as to the nature of the apparition remained unshaken. The experience had made a lasting impression on his mind and although he never willingly spoke of it, when he did it was always with great seriousness.

Among the many ghosts of Chillingham Castle in Northumberland includes that of a Radiant Boy who is said to haunt the Pink room and other parts of the private apartments of the owners. The ghost is said to call out, the eerie sound of his heart-rendering cries echoing through the corridors of the castle. During some restoration work in the 1920s the skeleton of a young boy wearing scraps of blue cloth was found in the walls of the building. The skeleton was taken away and given a Christian burial in a nearby church and apparently the Radiant Boy or Blue Boy stopped appearing after the burial although people still see unusual flashes of blue light in the room at night.

Angel Encounter

Do you believe in Guardian Angels? Many people do and although most believe Guardian Angels carry out their protective work without us knowing or realising, some say they can appear to us visibly either in their heavenly form or in human form, looking just like ordinary people. When Guardian Angels appear it is usually accompanied by a strong feeling of love, acceptance and peace. Some people might be visited by their Guardian Angel and they won't ever recognise it or know it. Others experience such wonder by the visit that they will remember it all their life.

Dennis doesn't believe in ghosts. Dennis doesn't believe in Guardian Angels. But the following incident has got him wondering .... Maybe, just maybe, Angel Encounters are possible.

Very sadly Dennis lost his wife, the love of his life of forty years, to Cancer. It was the lowest point of his life. He needed his wife and his daughter needed her mother. One day, while he was working in his daughter's cake shop a woman entered. It's difficult to say why or how this woman made a big impact on him because Dennis could only describe her as being dressed all in grey and looking sad. But she did make a big impression. She also reminded him of his wife. She walked up to Dennis and handed him a poem, telling him that it was for his daughter although she had scrubbed out the name. Dennis took the poem and when he looked up, the woman had vanished. His daughter had seen the woman too otherwise he could easily have believed the experience hadn't happened.

Some months later Dennis was in the shop and a woman came in. She was beautiful; her make-up was perfect, she was dressed smartly and she could have stepped out of the pages of a magazine. Somehow, although he can't explain how, Dennis knew this was the woman in grey who had visited before. The woman ordered two cups of coffee and sat down at the table where we were sitting as Dennis told me this story. She was sitting and Dennis wondered why two cups of coffee? Then a smartly dressed man came in and sat down beside her. These elegant visitors were very out of place in their little shop and yet somehow it seemed very natural that they should be sitting there.

Then the next time Dennis looked, the woman had disappeared. She hadn't walked past to go out of the door, no-one had left and no-one was walking away (the shop has a very open aspect at the front so it was easy to see people come and go). The man approached Dennis to pay for the coffee. He placed a load of money on the counter. Far too much! Dennis told him he couldn't accept it all and picked up the coins to put them back into the man's hand. His palm was facing up but as Dennis placed the coins into his hand, it bent almost 90 degrees back from the wrist (almost an impossibility for anyone to manage) so the coins spilled over the counter. Dennis reached to stop them, looked up and the man had vanished. There was no-one leaving the shop or walking away from the shop and no-one had gone out of the door. The man had just vanished.

Dennis does not believe in ghosts and yet he can't forget this experience. How had he known the female visitor was the same woman as the previous one when they looked so different? Why should such prestigious visitors enter their little shop and seem so at home there? Why hadn't he been offended by the man's actions when had it been another customer, he would have thought it very rude to have let the coins spill over the counter as he had done? How could both visitors have just vanished as they had done?

Could it be that when Dennis was feeling so down, he needed something to give him a little hope and reassurance? The gift offered was a special visit with enough about it that was strange and unreal to make it an unforgettable one and to cause Dennis to ponder over the reason.

The message offered by the noticeable change in the woman was to let Dennis know his wife wasn't sad anymore and neither should he be. She would always be alive in his heart. The gift of coins was also a message of protection for both Dennis and his daughter (the visit had taken place in his daughter's shop and she had witnessed both incidents).

Was Dennis touched by an Angel? Dennis does not believe in ghosts or Guardian Angels ... but this experience has him wondering!

Those who believe in Guardian Angels feel they are always near, ready to help and protect. This is usually invisibly but occasionally on very special occasions they will make themselves visible and often this is an experience that will remain with a person ... a sign of hope and reassurance ... for all their life.

Hotel Hauntings

"Crossroads" was a popular soap opera in England between the sixties and eighties, set in a fictional motel near Birmingham. The series was filmed in a number of locations and after the fictional hotel was destroyed by fire, the revamped Crossroads was filmed at the Golden Valley Hotel in Cheltenham.

And this is the setting of the next ghostly tale. Dave was on a course near the Golden Valley Hotel and had therefore booked into the hotel overnight. After an evening out with others on the course, they had a meal then returned to the hotel. Dave went to bed immediately and insists he hadn't been drinking. He fell asleep straight away but just past midnight he woke up for some reason and opened his eyes. Across the room, standing beside a table, was a woman in a long dress with a shawl wrapped around her head. She was looking at Dave and gave him a tentative smile as if he had surprised her by opening his eyes and seeing her when he shouldn't have. He kept his eyes fixed on her for quite a few seconds until she just faded away.

What surprised Dave most was that he did not feel spooked by the experience. The woman did not feel evil and if anything her presence was more of a warm and sisterly one. He had been awake because he used the bathroom after she disappeared and then went back to bed and fell asleep.

At the reception desk the next morning Dave asked whether there had been any reports of ghost-sightings in his room. The receptionist was intrigued by his tale and, keen on ghost stories encouraged him to tell her all. She hadn't heard any other reports like it but Dave still insists that he saw what he saw; he was awake and hadn't imagined it. Even though he can't explain it.

Many hotels in England are now claiming they have a reputation of being haunted. It is sometimes hard to distinguish which are serious claims and which are just jumping on the 'ghost-hunters' bandwagon. Ettington Park Hotel, a magnificent gothic mansion near Stratford-upon-Avon certainly looks the part. Almost any large gothic building can look spooky and this one may be ancient but it certainly isn't decaying. In fact it is incredibly grand. Up until the late 19th century the house belonged to the Shirley family who can proudly claim to be the only family in England whose lineage can be traced back by uninterrupted male descent for hundreds of years to the Domesday Book of 1086 and beyond.

Archaeological evidence suggests that a Roman villa once existed on this site as coins, ornaments and pottery were unearthed during an archaeological dig.

Through the centuries there have been a number of alterations and extensions to Ettington Manor as is often the case with ancient homes that remain standing. In the early 20th century the family moved to Ireland and for a while the house was leased to private individuals. In 1935 it was used as a nursing home and during the Second World War it served as a Prisoner of War camp for Italian prisoners. For a short while in the 1970s it was a night club and disco before a fire severely damaged the house in 1979. Prior to the fire it was used as a location for the film of Shirley Jackson's novel *The Haunting*. For three years the place was boarded up and left neglected until in 1983 the house was leased to a hotel company to eventually be opened as a luxury hotel after a massive restoration programme.

The house for the most part seems to have been loved and well maintained so could the ghosts that are said to haunt Ettington Manor be returning because of the happy memories associated with it? Or could it be that there is a message in the curse found in a battered book in its library of Sir Walter Scott's *Ronan's Well*. This book often falls off the shelf or is flung across the room always to fall open at the same page which states: "A merry place, 'tis said, in days of yore; But something ails it now, - the place is cursed."

A book falling off shelves is not the only paranormal goings-on in the library. There have been a number of reports of people having witnessed the phantom of a man and his dog wandering through the room before quickly vanishing.

Apparently, named the most haunted hotel in the UK by AA, there have been many reports of supernatural goings-on at Ettington Manor. Since it has been a hotel, both staff and guests have witnessed a range of supernatural phenomena including seeing phantoms, spectres and hearing disembodied voices.

As day turns to night and darkness starts to settle around the turrets of the old Gothic mansion, a grey lady has occasionally been seen by the great stone staircase. Her ghostly figure glides around the spot where it is said she met her death after having been pushed down the stairs. Another female phantom that drifts along the corridors of the hotel at dusk, scaring both guests and staff as she vanishes into the walls is that of a woman dressed in white. The staff of the mansion-now-hotel call this ghost Lady Emma, relating her to a governess who used to work for the Shirley family. Some think she is the same figure that is sometimes seen drifting along the cloister-like terrace dressed in a white flowing gown.

A ghostly woman dressed in Victorian clothing has also been seen and heard walking along the conservatory entrance.

Within the grounds of the hotel, the ghosts of two young boys wearing old-fashioned clothes have been seen. Guests have reported being woken up by the sound of a child crying outside their window. On looking out of the window, the guest saw the two ghostly figures staring pensively towards the river. It is believed that these are to young boys in the Shirley family who drowned in the Stour River in the 1800s.

One guest who was staying at the hotel in recent years heard a child's footsteps running up and down the corridor outside their room at around midnight. When the guest opened the door to look out into the hall, a young girl came running towards them. When the guest told her to go back to her room she passed directly through him and vanished into the wall.

There have also been sightings of a Monk both inside the hotel and in the grounds and an army officer while a number of staff are said to have witnessed a candle lift up off the mantelpiece in the library and float by itself. This occurred one Christmas Eve.

Haunted Boscastle Hotel

(Boscastle 1907 vintage postcard)

One of the world's largest collections of witchcraft related artefacts can be found in Boscastle in Cornwall. The museum's small rooms are cluttered with fascinating exhibits from those who practised the art of magic, some with a distinct satanic and malignant feel while others giving a fascinating glimpse into the beneficial side of white witchcraft. These witches, for instance, were practitioners of herbal medicine and home remedies. It was not 'spells' but remedies they would use to heal the sick. They knew that a drink made from catnip or chamomile would help relieve anxiety; a poultice made of mashed garlic plant would relieve the pain of a bee sting; peppermint, rosemary and sage helped ease headaches and garlic with honey was good for rheumatism. Many of these ancient remedies are still used today.

Is the Witchcraft museum in Boscastle haunted? Within this chamber of horrors there are instruments of torture that were used on those accused of practising witchcraft in England, many and most of them innocent, ordinary people whose lives were changed dramatically following these false accusations. There is a dark, spooky feel about the place, whether due to the nature of the artefacts of the possibility that it does house a ghost or two. Some visitors mentioned that when they went into the room that has the Ouija Board, the planchette pointed to 'No' when they went in. As they left around three-quarters-of-an-hour later, it was on 'Yes.' They had been the only visitors entering that room at the time.

(Boscastle 2011)

Visitors to Boscastle are more likely to receive a ghostly visit if they book into the Wellington Hotel. The hotel is believed to be haunted by a young girl who after being betrayed by her lover flung herself from the ramparts of the hotel's tower. Guests and staff have reported seeing a dark shape drift down the stairs late in the night to disappear into the cellar. Not just once but twice, retired policeman Bill

Searle saw a vague shape that seemed to be dressed in a cloak glide across the landing before going through the wall into a guest room.

At one time, Victor Torbutt, was at the reception desk when he looked up to see a figure of a man gliding past. When studying the figure in more detail, Mr Tobutt noticed that his hair was tied back in an old-fashioned style and he was wearing a frock coat, frilled shirt and leather gaiters and boots as would have been worn by an 18th century coachman. The figure looked incredibly solid and yet to the hotel owner's shock, it walked straight through a wall. When he described the experience to one of his employees, they too had seen this ghostly visitor a few times.

Brave guests might book into room number 9 which is reported to be the most haunted part of the building. So haunted, in fact, that a whole section of the hotel's information book is dedicated to the ghostly happenings in this room! A guest who stayed at the hotel left a comment on tripadvisor.com describing her experience in room nine:

"I was lying on the bed when suddenly I felt a really strange sensation and said to myself, 'Oh my God, it's here.' As those words ran through my mind I suddenly felt what can only be described as someone walking up the bed behind me and then a rush of cold air and then total paralysis of my body… I couldn't move I was frozen. I kept thinking if I can just reach the phone I can call my friend but I couldn't. This feeling lasted about 30 seconds and then as quickly as it came… it left me and I felt normal again."

It is also believed that a part of the hotel is haunted by a man who was murdered there while there is also a friendly animal spirit who was playfully pursued by the small dog of a hotel guest who was a writer of ghost stories. The writer himself did not see the ghost but his wife saw a shape move across the room followed by their excited dog, wagging its tail.

(A Boscastle Church Vintage Postcard 1920)

Minster Church in Boscastle stands alone, overlooking a wooded valley and like many old English churches stands among ancient tombstones overgrown with bracken and wildflowers. Within this site there is also a Pagan and later early Christian Healing Well. Both the Church and the well have a magical feel about them. It is believed they marked the place of an early cult around the Saint associated with nearby Tintagel. In the Middle Ages a small community of French Monks were established in this area. They could possibly have been spies during the 100 Years War. There are no remains of a monastery but the well is still standing.

Not many years ago Minster Church hosted the reinterment of the bones of a woman who was unjustly condemned as a witch in the 19th century. Especially as dusk descends, there is a heavy eeriness about this church, a solitary building standing in the middle of nowhere.

Not all Ghosts are Evil

What is it that fascinates people about ghosts and hauntings? Some are attracted to the horror element; it's the thought of experiencing a real-life horror movie that gets the juices flowing. Others take a more scientific approach, interested in researching and finding proof that ghosts actually do exist; certain that one day there will be absolute proof supporting supernatural phenomena. Whichever division they are interested in, paranormal investigations do get the adrenalin flowing: the heartbeat increases, palms sweat, skin temperature drops several degrees, blood pressure spikes and muscles tense.

For many, once drawn into the fascinating world of the paranormal, their passion cannot be extinguished. It isn't always the dark side of the supernatural that intrigues: the horror and evil associations with the paranormal. It is the divine division (guardian angels, helpful ghosts, miracles and celestial encounters) that can draw people as equally as strongly into the realms of the supernatural.

Everyone needs spirit power. A soul without spirit power would be like a car without an engine. It couldn't function. Some cultures believe that sources of spirit power include nature (the natural world around us) and the spirit world (ghosts, dreams, spiritual places). Good spirits can provide us with spirit power and it can be good to develop a healthy relationship with good spirits as this is one way to become a spiritually strong person. – This doesn't mean socialising with ghosts! - Just standing by the sea in silence and drawing in the positive spiritual energy or walking in the countryside can fill you with spirit power. The ancient Celts (our ancestors) had a strong affinity with nature and spirit power, recognising and respecting good spirits and malevolent ones.

Evil spirits, some believe, are entities that feed from someone else's spirit power.

So not all ghosts are evil and why should they be? After all, most souls are good and so in death why should they suddenly become malicious? There are haunted places that have a restful and calming atmosphere and there are tales of helpful ghosts such as the ghost of the nurse at the now demolished Hackney Hospital in London who walked the wards, tapping sleepy nurses on their shoulders to keep them from falling asleep on duty. Or the fairy in Lancashire known as Shrewfoot who saved a pedestrian from walking in front of a speeding lorry. There are probably as many good ghosts as malevolent ones who return to soothe, assist or warn others of impending danger.

References

Richardson I, "Records of a Quaker Family" West, Newman & Co. London (1899)

Rhys, Ernest, "The Haunters and the Haunted" London 1921

Western Morning news March 8 2005 "A Star turn in the Heart of the moor" Richard Austin Rhys, Ernest, ed. (1859–1946).

http://www.birminghamghosts.co.uk/#/lionel-and-patricia-fanthorpe/4549226349

http://www.thesun.co.uk/sol/homepage/news/3137865/Ghost-spotted-in-Cumbria-pub.html

http://www.oldandsold.com/articles32n/northumbria-19.shtml

http://www.mapit.kk5.org/#/stocksbridge-bypass/4545261240

http://metro.co.uk/2010/10/21/helpful-ghosts-and-shrewfoot-fairies-in-paranormal-hotspots-across-the-uk-555278/

http://www.handpickedhotels.co.uk/hotels/ettington-park-hotel/History/

Ghosts and Legends of Northumbria (Sandhill Press (1996))

Northumberland Haunted Houses

Matas, C "The Proof that Ghosts Exist", (Key Porter Books, 2008)

http://www.chillingham-castle.com/GhostsPg.asp?S=3&V=1&P=34

http://great-castles.com/chillinghamghost.php

http://www.hauntedcastlesandhotels.com/Scotland/eileandonan.htm

http://www.medieval-castle.com/haunted_castles_wales/gwyrch_castle.htm

http://www.bbc.co.uk/berkshire/content/articles/2005/10/12/windsor_castle_ghosts_feature.shtml

Author's article:
http://www.helium.com/items/2184188-most-popular-haunted-castles-in-the-uk-haunted-castles-in-scotland-and-ghostly-castles-in-wales

Visits and Guided Tours or talks to Guides at:
Chillingham Castle, Alnwick Castle, Bamburgh Castle, Lindisfarne Castle, Warkworth Castle, Tynemouth, Dumfries House, Gunsgreen House, Jamaica Inn

Interview with guest who participated in ghost hunt at the Schooner Hotel

http://www.chillinghamwildcattle.com/ghosts-history
http://www.culzeanexperience.org/education.asp?sub=2
http://www.secretbunker.co.uk/
http://www.sunderlandecho.com/community/nostalgia/retro/wearside-echoes-haunted-theatre-spooks-actors-1-3944289

Phillips Geog "Tyneside: Then and Now ISBN 0 9540174 2 0

http://www.hauntedplaces.co.uk/tynewear.htm

Pennington Pedigrees Volume 10-2, pages 1-12, Bob Sloan, October 1978.

Richardson I, "Records of a Quaker Family" West, Newman & Co. London (1899)

Rhys, Ernest, "The Haunters and the Haunted" London 1921

Western Morning news March 8 2005 "A Star turn in the Heart of the moor" Richard Austin Rhys, Ernest, ed. (1859–1946).

http://www.birminghamghosts.co.uk/#/lionel-and-patricia-fanthorpe/4549226349

http://www.thesun.co.uk/sol/homepage/news/3137865/Ghost-spotted-in-Cumbria-pub.html

http://www.oldandsold.com/articles32n/northumbria-19.shtml

http://www.mapit.kk5.org/#/stocksbridge-bypass/4545261240

http://metro.co.uk/2010/10/21/helpful-ghosts-and-shrewfoot-fairies-in-paranormal-hotspots-across-the-uk-555278/

http://www.handpickedhotels.co.uk/hotels/ettington-park-hotel/History/

Visits, Ghost Tours and Personal Interviews: Boscastle, Brampton, Carlisle Castle, Croglin, Seaton Delaval, Tully House, Tynemouth, Wetheral

Guided Tours and Visits to: Mary King's Close, Jedburgh Castle Jail, Muncaster Castle, Kielder Castle, Chillingham Castle, Culzean Castle

Personal Interview with guest attending ghost-hunt at The Schooner Hotel

Printed in Great Britain
by Amazon